Fresh-Squeezed Life Available Daily. Always Open. Come In!

Welcome

to the Fresh-Squeezed Life

Cafe

BRYNN TAYLOR ASHFORD

WestBow
PRESS

WestBow Press books may be ordered through booksellers or by contacting:

WestBow Press
A Division of Thomas Nelson
1663 Liberty Drive
Bloomington, IN 47403
www.westbowpress.com
1-(866) 928-1240

Because of the dynamic nature of the Internet, any Web addresses or links contained in this book may have changed since publication and may no longer be valid. The views expressed in this work are solely those of the author and do not necessarily reflect the views of the publisher, and the publisher hereby disclaims any responsibility for them.

ISBN: 978-1-4497-0278-6 (sc)
ISBN: 978-1-4497-0277-9 (e)

Library of Congress Control Number: 2010929968

Printed in the United States of America

WestBow Press rev. date: 8/12/2010

Welcome to the Fresh-Squeezed Life Cafe!

Introduction
to the Fresh-Squeezed Life Cafe

Have you been through hard times, and you don't want those hard times to define you, overwhelm you or to be the focus of your life?

Do you want to know how to cooperate with God as He purposes to use your hard times to glorify Him and bless others?

Do you long to be in a community of like-minded souls hungering for a deeper relationship with God and authentic relationships with others?

Do you want to be of some use to God in this world, drawing others to Him, blessing and inspiring others?

Welcome to the Fresh-Squeezed Life Cafe! Let's learn together how to enter into a life in Him that:

- receives supernatural life in the Spirit and lets it flow through us in devotion to Christ, and in the development of friendship and brotherly love (Acts 2:46);

- emphasizes learning from His Word how to live out God-honoring relationship, believing that there is no greater authority than God Himself on how to love Him and each other (I Timothy 4:16);

- becomes part of a serving community, blessing each other and those beyond our walls with our love made visible by loving action (James 2:14-18).

We recognize that:

Every thought becomes an inclination;
Every choice becomes a path; and,
Every path becomes a destination.

Join us as we choose Christ, and walk the path of life with joy, integrity and purpose. Welcome to the Fresh-Squeezed Life Cafe. Let's take the next step together.

Notes

Consider this book your resource to use in the way that is comfortable to you. You may want to read straight through and skip the questions the first time. You may choose to read independently, then discuss study questions together with your small group. You may choose to answer only a few questions at the end of each chapter.

If you are going through a trauma right now, or recovering from one, you may want to go through this book more than once. In that case, it can be helpful to use a different color ink each time you go through the book and answer questions, dating each ink color, so you can look back later and see your own growth.

I have included many questions, but don't let that overwhelm you. They are provided only as jumping off points for your own thinking as you walk with God and others on your journey. You may want to answer only a few questions after each chapter.

I would urge you to "come away" with Him every day, to focus on Him, listen to Him, read His Word and pour out your heart. This is where your healing is. This is where the life is.

I would love to hear about your experience with this book, whether you read it solo or with a group of Christian brothers and sisters. Please meet me at freshlifecafe.com and tell me your story. We are all in this together.

If you are leading a small group and using this book, you can pick up facilitator's guidelines at freshlifecafe.com as well.

May God abundantly bless and keep you.

Contents

Life: Its Squeezing

Life squeezes you. Sooner or later, it squeezes everybody. Do you feel as if you've been squeezed hard, wrung out like a dishcloth and thrown down by the difficulties of life? Life can squeeze the life right out of you! Sometimes it feels as if life is full of death, even if you stay alive, many little deaths. At times you may feel as if God Himself has abandoned you. David felt that way. "You have taken me up and thrown me aside...I wither away" (from Psalms 102:10-11). Then almost immediately we see David's hope and faith kick in, and he says, "You will arise and have compassion" (v.13). God always does.

In the meantime, when we feel like grapes in the winepress, it's hard to make sense of it all. How much bruising and crushing do we have to endure? What does it all mean? What is it all for? **What can you do when you feel as though all the life has been squeezed right out of you?**

When I was young and a new believer, I remember often being surprised and even shocked at what came out of me with a little squeezing. I still get those surprises, just not as often. Life's squeezing shows you what's in there, and it is not comfortable to see it, but it's necessary. *Oh. Not pretty. How can that be in me? But it is. Help me with that, God.* I can't fix what I refuse to admit is there. I must tell myself the truth about myself, even when it's not lovely.

Here's what I've learned: I must work at clinging harder to Christ, humbling myself to conform to His image, taking to heart God's heart revealed in His Word. When I hold tightly to Him, from Him I get sweetness and Life. Even when He reproves and corrects me, He does it with such tenderness and love, I can receive it as sweetness. No matter how hard I squeeze, what comes out of Him is His beauty in exchange for my ashes. No matter how angry I get, no matter how sick, no matter how sad, as I cling to Him His sweetness, His strength, His peace, His wisdom, His healing, His Life will pour out to me. I will never be the same, thank God. And He will always be the same, praise God.

So there are two kinds of squeezing going on here: The first kind is that life squeezes you and it hurts; that's a given, and you don't have a choice about most of it. The second is the Life you squeeze and wring out for yourself, the Gift already given, fresh-squeezed Life from God Himself, the Author of Life. You do have a choice here.

Here is the good news: Jesus Christ has come to give us Life, fresh-squeezed "life to the full" (John 10:10). Not just "barely getting by" life, although there will be times when that is what it is, and there's no point in putting a pretty bow on it and calling it something else. Life can be brutal, but *the Author of life has the power to reclaim what has been lost, redeem that which has a high price on it, heal what has been bruised, and exchange beauty for ashes. This is our God!*

And this is His invitation: **Dare to step into the Fresh-squeezed Life Cafe**. It's always open, the Light is always on, day and night. There He will meet you, and offer you what I am calling "fresh-squeezed Life" because you need to receive it fresh daily, and because you can have this Life even when life itself seems to be taking all the life right out of you. The secret to having this fresh-squeezed Life is to get connected, first to Him and then to His people, and after that get better connected. Drink Life itself, the kind of Life that becomes a well of living water springing up in you, and overflowing to others.

Most believers get just enough of this Life to get by, a sort of "frozen concentrated reconstituted" spiritual orange juice, a drive-through express-lane, Sunday-morning-religion stop-off on the way to the beach or the market, perhaps watching a few minutes of Christian television, or listening to Christian radio in the car on the way to work, or ritual prayers said before meals and bed. There is nothing wrong with any of this, but God wants so much more for you.

There is so much more nourishment, so much more Life, available. God invites you to squeeze the real, fresh oranges of spiritual Life every day; a little more work, it's true, but you'll be healthier over time, and you'll have the spiritual energy that spills over and offers Life to someone else. Nothing, not church services, not small group Bible study, not books of daily devotionals or Christian literature (though all of these are good and necessary), nothing takes the place of your own daily intimate relationship with Jesus Christ through the Word and prayer. *It's the connection that gives you Life*, and the connection is organic, requiring the flow of nourishment from the Vine, Christ, to the branch, the believer, every day, every moment.

This is real authentic relationship with the Creator of relationship, pressed into hard over a lifetime, in good times and in bad times. There are no special words, prayers, places or postures that make all this happen. We are not talking about magic formulas or even ritual prayers, as comforting and sometimes powerful as these may be.

There are, though, many prayers recorded in Scripture and handed down through years of church liturgy that are worth repeating, worth meditating on, and worth adopting as our own. We will take a look at some of these prayers, and make them our own.

The first and most important prayer, if you have not yet begun this journey of relationship with God, is to accept the free gift of Life that He offers you in Jesus Christ, just because He loves you, and just because you need it. If you do not yet believe He is the Son of God, sent to redeem you and adopt you as His own, I challenge you to start reading the Bible. Tell God simply, as you might a friend, "Help me to figure out what I believe about this. Help me to understand the truth about You." You might find yourself wanting to believe, but not believing. Pray along with

the man who begged Jesus to help his son who had terrible convulsions, "Help me overcome my unbelief" (Mark 9:24), and watch what God will do in you.

Before I accepted Christ, when I was resisting belief in him, I decided that I wanted to know the truth above all else, even if the truth was different than what I wanted it to be, even if it made me uncomfortable. It wasn't long before I was overwhelmed with the truth that Jesus is the Way to God; He is the Truth, and He is the Life. I feel certain that anyone who, above all, wants to know the truth, will find it in Him.

If you are ready to accept Christ into your life, you can be sure His love for you is limitless. "Come to me," he says, "all you who are weary and burdened, and I will give you rest. Take my yoke upon you and learn from me, for I am gentle and humble in heart, and you will find rest for your souls. For my yoke is easy and my burden is light" (Matthew 11:28-30).

Are you ready to put your trust in the One who created you, the One who knows you completely and loves you endlessly? Then don't wait. **Talk to Him right now**. Talk to Him as a Friend. Curl up on His lap and talk to Him as a loving Father. Bow before Him and acknowledge that He is holy, and you need His forgiveness and His help because you, on your own, are not and cannot be holy.

Use your own words, words that come from your own heart. Your tears, your words, your wordless prayers that you groan in your spirit when there are no words, are all precious to God. **You will not be turned away**. You will be welcomed into a big, loving family. God is our Father, Jesus our Savior and elder Brother, and we are all brothers and sisters attached to each other and to God in divine compassion, with the Holy Spirit as our constant companion and in-dwelling guide. **Welcome! Here, you are loved**.

Past Pain

1. How has life "squeezed the life out of you"? What have you been through that has been overwhelming?

2. What emotions did you have?

3. What decisions did you make?

4. How did these things change who you are?

5. Talk to God about all of this. Be honest. If you are mad at Him, tell Him so. He can handle it. If you need forgiveness, ask and receive. Whatever is on your heart, pour it out to Him now.

Pray this prayer adapted from Psalms 90:14-17: *Satisfy me in the morning with your unfailing love, that I may sing for joy and be glad all my days. Make me glad for as many days as I've been afflicted, for as many years as I've seen trouble. Let me see your work, and let my children also see your work. Show us your splendor. May your favor rest on us. Establish our work. Amen.*

Who Am I?

1. What words do you use to describe yourself that are different now, after going through hard times? (For example, you might think of yourself as a divorcee instead of a married person, or a victim of _____ or survivor of _____.) Write these words here:

2. How do you feel saying/writing those words: positive and empowered/encouraged, or helpless, hopeless and damaged?

3. You get to choose how to think of yourself. God says we are "more than overcomers" (Romans 8:37). We don't have to be victims! It has been said that in the presence of trouble, some people grow wings; others buy crutches. I want to be one that chooses wings, don't you? Write a new positive statement describing who you are, in the light of God's work in you.

4. Write down some of the hard-earned knowledge and wisdom you have gained because of these difficulties. You can now share this with others going through something similar.

5. List all the things you are grateful for in light of all these hard times. Read this list out loud to God as a prayer, a sacrifice of thanksgiving. Write it down. This is your own psalm!

Remind yourself over and over again throughout the day today: *"He does not ignore the cry of the afflicted"* (Psalms 9:12b). He hears you!

Who Am I Becoming?

The Author of life has the power to reclaim what has been lost, redeem that which has a high price on it, restore what has been bruised and what has been lost, and exchange beauty for ashes. This is our God!

1. What reclaiming, redeeming, restoring work has God already done in your life?

2. What reclaiming, redeeming, restoring work are you asking Him to do?

3. Write the story of how you came to know Christ.

4. Tell this story to someone this week. Encourage them to know that God loves them very much.

Tell how it went:

Talk to God, and tell Him what it means to you to be able to offer life and love in Him, to others going through hard times. Write your prayer here, then speak it out loud to your Father.

Our Power Source

1. List as many ways as you can think of for someone to know God better.

2. List what you do daily to know God better.

3. List what you do weekly to know God better.

4. Read Psalms 1. How often does David **read God's Word**, and **meditate** on it?

5. Read Psalms 5:1-3, Psalms 6:6-9, and Psalms 16:8. When does David **pray**?

6. Are you ready to step further into the Fresh-Squeezed Life Cafe? What will you do *today* to take a drink of God's fresh-squeezed Life?

7. *It's the connection that gives you Life, and the connection is organic, requiring the flow of nourishment from the Vine, Christ, to the branch, the believer, every day, every moment.*

Read John 15:1-8. What does this mean to you? Put it in your own words.

Courage on Our Journey

1. Read Psalms 19. Now read it out loud to God as a prayer. Write verse 14 on an index card or slip of paper. Keep it with you. Whenever you have a spare moment today, read that verse as a prayer to God. At the end of the day, tape it to your bathroom mirror and pray it each morning and evening. Share your experience with this.

2. *Life's squeezing shows you what's in there, and it may not be comfortable to see it, but it's necessary. Oh. Not pretty. How can that be in me? But it is. Help me with that, God. I can't fix what I refuse to admit is there. I must tell myself the truth about myself, even when it's not lovely.*

Are you sure you *really* want to know the truth about yourself? Talk to God about any fears, doubts or apprehension you have about admitting the truth and seeing it.

3. Read Psalms 32. What happened when David did not admit the truth about what was in his heart?

4. When he realized what he was doing, hiding sin in his heart, what was his decision?

5. How did this decision affect him?

6. Living a life of integrity is not for the faint of heart! Write your thoughts about these quotes:

"Pain nourishes courage. You can't be brave if you've only had wonderful things happen to you." (Mary Tyler Moore)

"Let us run with endurance the race that is set before us, fixing our eyes on Jesus." (Hebrews 12:1-2)

I Always Have a Choice

Eleanor Roosevelt once said, "You gain strength, courage, and confidence by every experience in which you really stop to look fear in the face. You are able to say to yourself, 'I lived through this horror. I can take the next thing that comes along. You must do the thing you think you cannot do."

II Corinthians 1:3-4 says, *"What a wonderful God we have, who so wonderfully comforts and strengthens us in our hardships and trials. And why does he do this? So that when others are troubled, needing our sympathy and encouragement, we can pass on to them this same help and comfort God has given us."*

HENRY BURTON WROTE. HAVE YOU HAD A KINDNESS SHOWN? PASS IT ON.
TWAS NOT GIVEN FOR THEE ALONE. PASS IT ON.
LET IT TRAVEL DOWN THE YEARS.
LET IT WIPE ANOTHER'S TEARS.
TILL IN HEAVEN THE DEED APPEARS——PASS IT ON.

Henry van Dyke observed, "Happiness is inward, and not outward; and so it does not depend on what we have, but on what we are."

Considering these quotes, write your own thoughts on the choices you make every day about small and large things. Your choices add up to be a path; your path is really also a destination. Who are you, and where are you going? Sometimes we can feel swept along by the pace of life or circumstances beyond our control. Focus for a moment on what you do have control of, your own choices each moment. God has granted us both the right and the ability to make our own choices. It's a big responsibility, but it's also an exciting opportunity. You do have a choice!

You may not have a choice about being squeezed in the winepress of life, but you can choose to be the kind of grapes that release sweet, life-giving juice to others. Meditate on this as you squeeze some orange juice (or other fresh juice) right now; take a big, refreshing drink. Thank God that He will teach you and enable you, as you migrate out of misery into mission.

Choices: Migrating out of Misery

A whole book has been written about the prayer of Jabez. It is a prayer worth paying attention to, but one that could easily be overlooked. It is tucked away in several pages of genealogy in I Chronicles, pages that are dry reading for most of us, ones we gladly skip. But don't skip this. Out of lists and lists of names, the chronicler stops to spend a paragraph on Jabez. Something was noteworthy about this man.

The only reason we know his name today is because of a prayer he prayed, recorded in I Chronicles 4:9-10. The birth of Jabez was unusually painful. Both mother and child survived, but Jabez must have grown up hearing the story of his birth, and the explanation for his name, "Jabez" meaning "pain" or "misery." The pain experienced may have been either emotional or physical, or both; we aren't told. All we know is that this was not a happy time. Jabez was born in misery, and every time his mother called him by name, they were both reminded of it.

Here is the great thing about Jabez to me: he didn't accept that he was destined for misery. He didn't want these sad stories of his beginnings to be the continuing story of his life. He didn't just passively hope that things would get better, or work frantically to fix it on his own. He passionately pursued a relationship with God that would enable him to lay hold of God's blessing, presence, and productivity.

Jabez didn't just calmly bow his head in temple one day and say to himself, "I sure hope God will hear me and bless me." **He asked *passionately*:** He "cried out." He knew he was in desperate need of a change in his life. Forget about being "proper," or "refined." Jabez cared more about authenticity than he did about appearances. He fell apart before God.

He asked *pointedly*: He told God exactly what he wanted. First, he wanted God's blessing. He wanted to leave a legacy of an "enlarged territory" for the next generation. He wanted to be productive, to see that his life counted for something.

And then he prayed an extremely insightful and wise prayer: "Keep me from harm so that I will be free from pain." All his life he had heard the family stories, that his birth, his life and his name were all about pain. *Jabez refused to be a victim.* He went to the only One with the power to break the cycles of pain, victimhood and woundedness. And God granted his request. The cycle was broken. This is a miracle, and it is a miracle available to all of us.

We all have wounded places within us. When we put our own Band-Aids on them and keep going, no matter how hard we try to avoid it, life keeps jabbing at those sore spots. It hurts. The infection that has built up oozes out. We think, *That's ugly. I'm not like that; that can't be part of me.* We cover it back over and pretend it's not there. But here's the thing: It doesn't work. It never works.

Healing of a wound requires exposure to light and air. First we have to see what we're dealing with. We have to look at it in all its ugliness and call it what it is. That's what Jabez did. He gave it a name. He called it what it was: pain and misery.

Instead of pretending it wasn't there, or that it wasn't that bad, or that he could handle it on his own, he acknowledged that he desperately needed help. He went to the Great Physician. He was ready to learn how to stay out of harm's way so that he wouldn't keep experiencing this terrific pain. He cried out to God, and God granted his request.

He asked *publicly*. We'd rather not think about this. We try to hide our not-so-nice parts from others. We don't want to be judged. It scares us to be fully known. Yet God says, "Confess your sins to each other and pray for each other so that you may be healed. The prayer of a righteous man is powerful and effective" (James 5:16). God's ways are not our ways. He intends for us to be in transparent, transformational relationship with Him and with each other. To get there, we have to be willing to be honest with each other about who we really are, and who we are struggling to become.

"Keep me from harm so that I will be free from pain." This is what Jabez prayed. We, on the other hand, sometimes think it is far more spiritual to experience pain in this life, so we accept all pain that comes our way. There is, of course, a certain amount of pain we will all experience in this world. We gain wisdom when we confess our pain to other believers who have walked through pain; they can help us discern whether this is pain to "walk through" or pain to "fight our way through."

There is pain that results from our own sins, mistakes, blind spots and our failure to depend on God. This pain is logical and natural; God has built it into the natural order of things. It is meant to give us an opportunity to learn to do better. It hurts, but it is supposed to work for our good. This kind of pain will "grow us up" if we let it.

There is harm we suffer at the hands of others, because of their sins, mistakes, blind spots and independence from God. They may hurt us intentionally or unintentionally, but either way the damage can be deep and lasting. Nothing that originates from sin is God's will, so none of this can be said to originate with God.

Yet God can redeem anything. Joseph, upon being reunited with the brothers who had sold him into slavery, told them, in effect, You meant it for harm, but God meant it for good (The whole story is in Genesis 37-45). We can go through terrible undeserved suffering at the hands of others, and if they intend evil toward us, the suffering and grief we feel are even more intense. *God can use even this for our good, if we let Him.*

There is also the suffering inherent in living in a world that groans for redemption from its "bondage to decay" (Romans 8:20-22). Suffering may come in the form of cancer, loss of a job, loss of a loved one or a lifetime of caring for a special needs child. Nobody's out to get you. You didn't do anything to cause these troubles and challenges. They are part of living in a very imperfect world. Everyone is touched by them in one form or another.

Some suffering comes as an attack straight from the pit of Hell; this is pain we need to recognize as an attack and fight against. We have a very real adversary, and we need to do battle every day, confident in God's promise that "no weapon forged against us shall prevail" (Isaiah 54:17). We should not accept these attacks as our due; we are to be harmless as doves, but wise as snakes (Matthew 10:16). We need to see these attacks for what they are, and not submit to them. God always wins in the end, if we cling to Him as our One Sure Thing. Our part is to "put on the full armor of God" (Ephesians 6:11-18), "resist the devil, and he will flee" (James 4:7).

How do we know whether our suffering is something to accept or fight? We need wisdom! There are so many ways suffering comes and so many sources of evil. We need to know how to avoid harm, and we also need that utter dependence on God that says, *No matter how discerning and emotionally healthy I get, I still can't keep myself from harm. God, I need You to keep me from harm.* We need to pray a prayer like the one Jabez prayed: *Lord, keep me from evil, that I may be free from unnecessary pain.*

Many years after Jabez lived, Jesus taught his disciples to pray, "Deliver us from evil" (Luke 11:4). *This is a God-breathed prayer.* If we spend our lives overwhelmed by the evil in ourselves and the evil in the world around us, we won't have the time and energy to spend on developing full meaningful relationships with God and others; we will be so focused on dealing with our own emergencies, we won't be available to help others with theirs. God's kingdom will have lost a willing worker. We need to pray, *Deliver us from evil!*

Though we all have troubles, we want to learn how to avoid trouble that's avoidable, and triumphantly make it through trouble that's not. We want to be living that good life that God has planned for us, so that we have something to give others. We want our lives to show others the beauty of having a relationship with God, so they will want that for themselves.

Ernest Hemingway wrote, "Life breaks us all. Afterward some are stronger at the broken places."

"The Lord is close to the brokenhearted and saves those who are crushed in spirit" (Psalms 34:18).

God can mend a broken heart, but we have to give Him all the pieces.

This is what I know: No matter what happens to you, you do not have to be a victim. Feel your pain, cry your tears, yell out those angry or hurt prayers to God, and then submit yourself to the Great Physician, who knows how to do life-saving surgery and how to work all things together for your good. He will make you stronger in the broken places. Just let Him do the work. Amen. Let it be so.

Pray Passionately

1. Read I Chronicles 4:9-10. Close your eyes and imagine Jabez coming to the end of his rope and crying out to God with passion and emotion. What might he have done when he felt that way? How do you imagine him?

2. Have you ever been at the end of your rope? What were the troubles that brought you to that place of desperation?

3. What did you do?

4. What was the result?

5. Read Jabez's prayer again. This time, re-write it, using words you would naturally use. Make this a passionate prayer and make it your own. It does not have to be beautifully eloquent. Let it come from the deepest place of desperation, weakness and need within you. Copy or type it onto an index card and take it with you wherever you go this week. Whenever you have a spare moment, take it out, and pray it silently. Pray it when you first open your eyes in the morning, and the last thing before you close your eyes at night. *Try this!*

Pray Pointedly

1. Take a look at the prayer you previously created. Is your prayer "pointed," that is, specific?

Are you being very clear with yourself and with God what you are asking for?

2. List exactly what you want from God.

    a.

    b.

    c.

3. Double-check your prayer. Does it specifically ask for these things?
   If not, go back now and make the additions and changes you want to make.

4. When God answers this prayer, will it be obvious?

Explain how.

Take a moment now to meditate on the wonderful truth that God honored the simple prayer of Jabez, and that He wants to bless us and keep us from harm. What a good God He is! Spend some time thanking Him.

"You have loved back my life from the pit of nothingness and corruption."
(Isaiah 38:17, Amplified)

Going Public

1. You have read the prayer of Jabez. You have created your own prayer asking for freedom from harm. You have made it passionate and pointed. Now for the "public" part. Tell someone exactly what you are praying for. Choose someone you trust and if this is confidential, be sure to make that plain. Who did you tell?

   How did you feel about doing this?

2. Now that you have read and prayed this prayer, make any changes to it you want to make, title it "The Prayer of (your name)" and type it in a font you like, or do your own calligraphy. Make a Bible bookmark out of it, or frame it, or whatever helps you to honor your own quest to move into that fresh-squeezed "life to the full" God intends for you. Take the time to do this.

3. What are some of the "Band-Aid"s you've put on your own wounds? (for example, staying busy, accomplishing things, addictions, serial relationships)

   How did they work?

We can go through terrible undeserved suffering at the hands of others...God can use even this for our good, if we let Him.

4. What is your reaction to this statement?

What do you think is necessary in order for this to happen?

5. What kind of relationship is it possible to have with someone who has deeply wounded us?

An Action Plan for Adversity

1. Read Matthew 10:16. What does it mean to be harmless as doves, wise as snakes?

2. Read James 4:7. What does it mean to "resist the devil"?

3. What are some ways you can discern the source of the evil you experience?

4. Decide on an "action plan" to prepare for and deal with/fight adversity when it occurs in your life. Write it down here. Be specific. Pray about this as you work.

Stronger at the Broken Places

Ernest Hemingway wrote, "Life breaks us all. Afterward some are stronger at the broken places."

1. Do you agree with the above quote? Explain.

2. Read Ephesians 6:11-18. How in practical terms can you put on the whole armor of God, so that you can stand against the attacks of the enemy? Explain specifically what you can do, when, how, etc.

3. How important do you think this is?

Explain why.

Albert Einstein once said, "In the middle of difficulty lies opportunity." Think of your troubles as an opportunity to learn greater dependence on God, and to understand His plan and will better. Ask God to make you stronger at the broken places, and thank Him for His heart toward you, the heart of a compassionate Father.

"He knows the way that I take. When he has tested me I will come forth as gold." (Job 23:10)

Always a Choice

What are the steps that you personally can take to recover from wounds of the past and move into the greater spiritual, emotional and physical health that God wants for you, and that you want for yourself? Be very specific. Approach this prayerfully. Add this to your action plan. Write it down here:

"I found myself in trouble and went looking for my Lord; my life was an open wound that wouldn't heal. O God! Your way is holy! You're the God who makes things happen. You pull your people out of the worst kind of trouble."

(from Psalms 77:2, 13-15)

Life: Its Price

Love is Costly

This Life, this fresh-squeezed Life, is freely available to you, but oh so costly. It cost God the Father the suffering, death and separation of His beloved Son. It cost God the Son his earthly human life and gruesome death, giving up Heaven for a time, unimaginable suffering, both physical and emotional, and excruciating spiritual suffering; His Father turned away from looking at the sins of the world in all their enormity and depravity, the sins that the Father Himself had placed on Him to carry. Whatever we have lost or suffered, Jesus experienced that and infinitely more.

Whatever betrayals, whatever unjustified fury and judgment we have endured against us, Jesus endured more. Whatever the painful, shameful, humiliating sins we have committed or have been committed against us, Jesus carried the weight of all that and more on the Cross. His life was squeezed out in physical torture, emotional agony, degradation and aloneness that day; the price for the fresh-squeezed Life to the full He offers us cost Him everything.

And yet when His life was squeezed out, Life, sweet, forgiving and abundant, poured out of Jesus; Love, crucified, only poured out more and more Love. Love is the reason **He was willing to pay the price of suffering for us to have Life**. He loves us *that much*.

This means that your suffering is important to God; Jesus knows what it's like to be human and to suffer. He has compassion on us in our suffering. Paul, in Hebrews 2, reminds us that Jesus experienced being reduced from divinity to humanity, and in His humanity went through temptation, suffering, and death. He is the author of our salvation, now crowned with glory and honor *because* he suffered. Because he suffered, we are made holy, and because He suffered, He has become our brother.

"Because he himself suffered when he was tempted, he is able to help those who are being tempted. Therefore, holy brothers [and sisters], who share in the heavenly calling, fix your thoughts on Jesus" (Hebrews 2:18-3:1). "For we do not have a high priest who is unable to sympathize with our weaknesses, but we have one who has been tempted in every way, just as we are, yet without sin. Let us then approach the throne of grace with confidence, that we may receive mercy and find grace to help us in our time of need" (Hebrews 4:15-16).

This Life available to us in Him is the way of love. Has love cost you? Perhaps loving someone has cost you dearly and unfairly. You are in good company; Jesus has walked this road before you. Hopefully, learning to love has widened your heart, deepened your character, and taught you things you would not have learned any other way. Love is costly, yet it also works good stuff within us, if we stay open and pliable in God's hands. Accept the cost love has demanded from you, even if the relationship no longer exists. God can redeem anything, if we allow it.

Love Gives and Receives

There is a danger that our suffering will cause us to develop a tough shell in an attempt to protect ourselves from further hurt. "See to it that none of you has a sinful, unbelieving heart that turns away from the living God. But encourage one another daily, as long as it is called Today, so that none of you may be hardened. Today if you hear his voice, do not harden your hearts" (Hebrews 3:12-15). A suffering heart sometimes becomes a hardened heart, in an attempt to stop the suffering. A hardened heart will commit the sin of unbelief.

If you have gone through deep suffering and grief and you feel broken open, *let it be*. **Into that brokenness, God can and will pour His love and grace and mercy** to overflowing, so that there is enough to bless, not only you but, those around you through your humble brokenness and openness to God. He pours in sweetness and out it flows from you to others.

If something else is flowing out, notice it. This is an area of hardness of heart, a place in need of healing. Don't close it off because it's painful. Open it up to Him, and let the sweetness and tenderness of God flow into that broken place. Just as pouring disinfectant into an open wound makes you cry out, this will too. You will cry and rage out all the pain from that place, and God will heal you. Trust Him with your raw, tender, broken places; do not shut Him out.

If we won't receive God's love and healing, we can see love, we can imitate it, convince others that we have it, even convince ourselves that we have it, but that's not the same as truly experiencing it. And without experiencing it, we don't have it to give. This Christ-like, life-giving love is ours to give *only* if we have first received it from God.

Many people find it easier and happier and more acceptable to give than to receive. *This looks spiritual, but it's not.* While it's more blessed to give than to receive, it is also necessary to receive what we do not have, so that we have it to give. We must admit that in ourselves what we have to give is terribly and terminally insufficient. It's not just that we don't have *enough* love or patience or mercy, we don't even have the *right* stuff. Jesus told us to love others *just like he loves us* (John 13.34). We cannot do that on our own. We are made of different stuff. We must learn to become dependent on God.

We must experience that tender divine love toward us before we know how to give it away. It is a lifelong process to learn how to let God give love to us in every area of our minds, hearts, hurts and memories. As we let Him in, He loves and heals, and we learn yet another way to love others. If we don't fully let Him in, to that extent we will be hobbled in our ability to love one another.

If we hide our most unlovely parts from Him and refuse to let Him love us in all our astonishing inadequacy, we will be unable to love others in their insufficiency.

When we find ourselves being harsh and judgmental, let it be a spiritual red flag, warning us to go into a private prayer time with God, where we wrestle with whatever it is we are holding onto, whatever it is God wants to heal, and to let go of it into the hands of God.

We can't be fully connected to God if we are cutting off the flow of life to essential parts of us. Jesus says, "I am the vine; you are the branches. If you remain in me and I in you, you will bear much fruit; apart from me you can do nothing" (John 15:5). *Nothing!*

Don't you want to tap into that Vine? And not just tap in, but be so connected that you are one with the Vine, the life of the Vine flowing freely through you? I do! To the degree that we press in and learn to be connected to Him, dependent on His life flowing through us, to that extent will we function in the Body of Christ as God intends, and to that extent will we understand and begin to live out the principles of godly relationships, and to that extent will we produce good fruit.

It is also necessary that healthy relationships with each other involve both giving and receiving, not that one person is the primary giver and the other is the primary receiver, but that both people are comfortable with both giving and receiving. There is a vulnerability about being willing to receive, to admit we need prayer, to ask for help, to ask for forgiveness, and we need to be willing to do these things. Since it is more blessed to give than to receive, we need to extend that blessing to others in our lives, and allow them to give to us when we need it.

So Life, and the Love that it both springs from and produces, are costly, and that Life, that Love, requires *both* giving and receiving. Are you willing to receive as well as give?

Love Holds Itself Accountable

Even though Jesus was so desperate to avoid the horrible suffering that was before Him as He faced the Cross, that he prayed to His Father to spare Him, nevertheless He went through with it. This was the plan, the remedy for this sin-sick world, and He had already agreed to it. He held himself accountable to do His part. He loves His Father, and He loves us, *that much.*

Do we hold ourselves accountable, or do we make excuses, shrug off our lapses with, "I'm only human"? God's Word never seems to suggest that this is OK. Although forgiveness is always there when we repent, **God's standard, the goal for which we aim, is amazingly high**: "Be perfect as your heavenly Father is perfect" (Matthew 5:48). We are accountable to God for what we do with His Word.

Love Tells the Truth

This Fresh-Squeezed Life, this Love lived out, demands truth-telling. God didn't just gloss over our rebellion against Him and call it something nicer, as we like to do, putting a positive spin on nearly everything. He didn't call it "too smart for their own good," or "spunky," or "hilariously irreverent." He called it what it was: "desperately wicked" and "wounded."* It is important to admit there is a problem and then to name the problem correctly, or you will never find a solution. God acted to secure our redemption because He saw clearly the deadly serious nature and consequences of sin, and called it what it was. Love tells the truth. He loved us enough to tell us the ugly truth about our condition.

And so **we must be courageous and face the truth** about ourselves. Does the truth feel harsh? Does telling yourself the truth feel like venturing out onto a high wire at the circus? Pray along with David, "When I said, 'My foot is slipping, your love, O Lord, supported me. When anxiety was great within me, your consolation brought joy to my soul' (Psalms 94:18-19).

God's grace is the safety net into which you can fall again and again. God will never stop loving you; you must step out over the darkness, and trust that God will catch you.

* Jeremiah 17:9: *The heart is deceitful [aqob] (crooked, polluted) above all things, and beyond cure [anash] (frail, feeble, melancholy, desperate, sick, woeful).*

Love is Costly

1. This fresh-squeezed life has come at a high price. God was willing to pay it because He loves us so much. Have you ever loved someone so much you were willing to pay a high price for their good? What acts of love did it produce in you?

2. What fruit did those acts of love produce?

3. Do you think God wants to see good fruit produced in your life because he paid such a high price for you? What good fruit is God seeing in your life now?

   What good fruit do you think He is still waiting for?

4. We are to "fix our eyes on Jesus" and "approach the throne with confidence," when we are going through trials, when we need forgiveness, when we need an answer to prayer. Do you do both of these things?

   If not, what holds you back?

5. What has love for God or others cost you?

   How do you feel about that?

Can you accept that, even if it's been very costly for you to love, even if the results don't seem worth it, God can use all of it for His glory, if you keep your heart from being hardened?

Pray about all of this, asking for God's intervention to reveal truth and heal any bitterness.

Love Gives and Receives

1. Love both gives and receives. Even God both gives and receives. What have you first received and then been able to give?

2. Think of a time when a part of your heart was hardened. Did it keep you from receiving from God and others? Explain.

3. How do you think a broken heart can harden your heart and make it difficult for you to give and receive?

4. How do you think a broken heart can widen your heart and make it easier for you to give and receive?

5. True giving and receiving requires honesty, openness and "softness," or vulnerability. Stop for a moment and ask God to show you any areas of your life where you are playing a role instead of really living it from the inside out. Do you "play church," going through the motions, but not really entering into worship? Do you "play at relationship," doing and saying things that make another person feel cared about, yet knowing you are not being completely honest?

These are areas that God can heal and develop into strengths, but only with your passion and perseverance to cooperate with Him in this. What is your choice?

Imagine you are holding your own heart in both your hands. Handle it gently. Notice the imperfections, the damaged places, toughened over with protections against further hurt. Look kindly on your own heart. Raise it above your head as an offering. Ask God to heal and strengthen the broken places. Ask Him to widen and soften your heart.

"Pour out your heart like water in the presence of the Lord." (Lamentations 2:19)

Love Holds Itself Accountable

1. What areas of your life are "off limits" to God?

2. What unlovely parts of you do you hide or deny with God?

   With others?

   With yourself?

3. Think of a relationship or situation in which you were, or are, harsh or judgmental. Confess this to God in prayer now, release the guilt and self-condemnation, and receive God's forgiveness. Ask Him if there is anything you need to do to repair any damage.

4. Being vulnerable and admitting to others when you need help, prayer or forgiveness allows others the blessing of being able to give to you. Is this easy or hard for you?

5. Being needy can make others feel needed, but it requires them to give much more than they receive in a relationship. How true is this of you?

Confess to God your inability to give and forgive. Invite Him to do His work in you.

Accountability in Relationship

1. Love is accountable; that is, it holds itself responsible for a certain standard of conduct and attitude. Think of a relationship that you now have. What do you hold yourself accountable for in this relationship?

2. What do you hold the other person accountable for?

3. 3. Is there mutual accountability in this relationship, i.e., do you both hold each other accountable? How is that done?

4. Accountability depends on both trust and submission. Explain. (You may want to read Ephesians 5:21 and I Corinthians 1:10.)

Love Tells the Truth

1. Love tells the truth. Without naming names, describe a time when you were disappointed by deception in a relationship.

   How did that experience affect you?

   How did you handle it at the time, or when you learned of the deception?

2. Describe a time when you yourself did not live up to this standard of telling the truth in love.

   Why did you make this choice?

   What was the result? How did you feel about it?

   What did you learn? Decide?

Telling the truth is sometimes very difficult. We don't want to deal with the consequences of being honest. Telling the truth takes courage and character. Ask God to help you in this area.

Love is a Choice

1. Which of these areas (the cost/sacrifice/inconvenience of relationship; receiving; giving; being accountable; telling the truth) is most difficult for you?

2. What difficulties have you experienced in this area?

3. In which of these areas have you done the most "pretending," that is, acting "as if" instead of its springing from your heart?

4. Make a decision about the kind of person you want to be in relationships, and in your relationship with God. Are you willing to pay the price, to sometimes give up what you want?

   Are you willing to admit to someone else how you are really feeling, what you want or need, and then be open to receiving something from the other person?

   Are you willing to be accountable to God, to yourself, to another person for your actions? To apologize, if necessary?

   Are you willing to tell the truth?

   Are you willing to hear the truth?

Every thought is an inclination; every choice, a path; every path, a destination. Spend some time in prayer, being honest with God about how you really feel and where you are in this area of relationships. Look honestly at where you've been and where you want to go. Remember, God can redeem anything! Ask Him for his help in your areas of weakness. Make a commitment to Him about what you will do to make progress toward loving the way God loves.

Love: The Invitation

This is what God's love is like:

God's love for us costs Him.

God's love gives and also receives.

Unbelievably, God holds Himself accountable. He's the king of the universe, he can do whatever he wants, yet he holds himself accountable to his promises and to his nature.

God's love is based on the truth.

That's what love looks like on God. What does it look like on us?

Love is *costly.*

Love is *both giving and receiving.*

Love is *accountable.*

Love is *based on the truth.*

One place in scripture we see this lived out in real life by an ordinary human being is in I Chronicles 21. David has sinned by ordering a census of his considerable military might, acting out of his own wisdom and pride, instead of trusting that God will be Israel's defender from the surrounding nations. The judgment of God against him is severe, and all Israel experiences the deadly consequences: a plague that kills many of the troops David had so proudly numbered in the census. David cries out in repentance to God (verse 17), "I am the one who has sinned. Let your hand fall on me." After watching others suffer and die as a result of his own sin, his heart is grieved. He is willing to be *accountable* for his own sin, willing to bear the results without dragging everyone else down with him. A sense of personal accountability based on conscience comes from the ability to imagine what it's like to be someone else. **When we realize someone else is suffering pain just as we have suffered pain, we have compassion on them. This is at the heart of love.**

In verse 24, David buys Araunah's threshing floor to turn it into an altar where he will call on God to seek forgiveness and an end to the plague. He refuses to take the threshing floor as a gift, saying to Araunah, "I will not take for the Lord what is yours, or sacrifice what costs me nothing." He understands that love is costly, and he is *willing to pay the cost.*

"So David built an altar and sacrificed and called on the Lord and the Lord answered him" (verse 26). In this verse we see that David gave and he received. The free flow of that Life was available to him, because he was open and not closed. God had punished him. David was painfully aware of his own sin. In relationships with God and others, how often does this cause us to close up and shut down? David *understood and lived out this openness of both giving to and receiving from God and others.* Because of this, he was called by God "a man after God's own heart," and he had Life flowing through him, in spite of his sometimes terrible sins.

David *recognized and admitted the truth,* even when it revealed him to be a sinner of the worst sort. In this incident, the result of that honesty with himself is shown by his reaction to God's punishment for David's sin. Even though there was a tabernacle available to David, he didn't go there because "he was afraid of the sword of the angel of the Lord" (verse 30). The divine punishment, for David's sin of looking to his troops instead of to God for victory in war, was devastating: 70,000 men dead of the plague, before David begged for the punishment to be on him and not on all of Israel. David knew that he deserved even more punishment. He felt godly fear based on this truth, a fear that created humility, dependence and an awareness that he was in a relationship with a holy God.

He was living B.C., before Christ, before the veil separating God and man had been torn, before the Cross had once for all atoned for the enormity of each individual's sin, by mediating "a better covenant." Before Christ, "the gifts and sacrifices being offered were not able to clear the conscience of the worshiper" (Hebrews 9:9), and David felt this. Christ paid a very high price for us when we were on the auction block with Satan as the only other bidder; His death gives us the assurance that, covered by His blood, we can safely approach the throne of the Most High God.

For us, on this side of the Cross, we no longer fear that God will continue to strike us down for our sin, once we have sincerely repented of it, *but we need to be aware that we still deserve it.* God is still God, and the moment we depend on our own goodness instead of Christ's righteousness, we have lost touch with who we are and to Whom we are accountable. When the Messiah walked this earth, He was severe with the religious elite, the ones who were confident of their own goodness. They were out of touch with the truth about themselves. Let's not follow their path.

The *only* way we can "walk humbly before our God" is to be a truthteller. The truth is that God is good and merciful, but He is also just, jealous and all-powerful. The truth is that we are totally dependent on Him for everything good, even our next breath. No wonder Paul exhorts us to "work out our own salvation with fear and trembling" (Philippians 2:12).

We serve the same God that David knew; he has not changed. Of Him, David said, "Serve the Lord with fear and rejoice with trembling. Kiss the Son, lest he be angry and you be destroyed in your way, for his wrath can flare up in a moment. Blessed are all who take refuge in him" (Psalms 2:11-12).

The Invitation

The way then to this Fresh-Squeezed Life is through Love: love relationships with God and others. Love is costly, even sacrificial. Love is accountable, and it holds itself accountable because, in good conscience, it wants to bring joy not sorrow to others and to God; in other words, this accountability springs from compassion. Love is open and reciprocal, both giving and receiving. Love is truthful. It is before us a vast ocean of unknowns and possibilities.

I live near the Pacific Ocean, but I've never been out swimming in it. Physically, I'm just not a strong enough swimmer. And guess what? I'm not a strong enough swimmer to stay afloat in this ocean either.

The Good News is that God Himself will teach me how to swim in this spiritual ocean. I can't learn to swim if I won't get in the water. Neither will you.

God extends continually to each one of us an invitation to join Him in this adventure of a Fresh-Squeezed Life lived out with Love.

Let's dive in.

Accountability starts with Compassion

1. David became fully accountable for his own sin when he looked at others and realized the price they were paying because he had disobeyed God. Looking at others and truly seeing them is where deep, compassionate, Christ-like Love begins. Read Luke 7:11-17. What feelings and attitudes did Jesus have toward the mother?

   How do you know? In what ways did He show that He really understood?

2. First Jesus had to look at her, and see her. This is where Love starts, by really seeing. When you truly see someone, you are able to put yourself in that person's place, and feel what they feel. Do you think you usually truly see people in your family?

   People in your church?

   People you don't know?

3. Describe a time that you had compassion on someone, a time when you were "moved to compassion," as Jesus was in this incident.

   What effect did this have on you?

4. When someone tells you they are unhappy with you, how do you respond?

   How could greater compassion help you do better in these situations?

5. How could you use the times that you fall short to become both more accountable, and more compassionate?

6. How does being truly compassionate result in truly holding yourself accountable?

Paying the Cost of Love

1. There are many sayings that reflect the basic truth that something of value is going to cost you something. "There is no free lunch." "You get what you pay for." Many people get married, develop friendships, or join a church without understanding this basic concept: *A relationship is going to cost you.* When it is necessary to give up what they want to do, or perhaps to listen, or to change the way they do something in order to accommodate the other person, they are offended. Think of a time when you experienced a conflict in a relationship at home, at work, in the neighborhood or at church. Describe exactly what the problem was.

   How did you react?

   What was the result?

   What can you learn from this incident?

2. Write a definition of love.

3. What did God's love for us cost him?

4. Why did David refuse to accept Araunah's gift of the threshing floor, and insist on paying top dollar for it?

5. What does this story illustrate about the significance of being willing to "pay the price" of love?

Spend some time in prayer, thanking God that He was willing to pay the price for your sin, so that you could enter into a love relationship with Him.

Openness to Giving and Receiving

1. The character trait of openness includes an *attitude* of honesty, as well as the *behavior* of communication. These are both helpful in authentic giving and receiving. Read Proverbs 27:5-6. Explain in your own words the difference between openness and its opposite.

2. Read Ezekiel 2:1-8. How did God require openness from Ezekiel? What was he to receive?

   What was he to give?

3. Read Revelation 3:19-22. What is being given?

   What needs to be given?

   What needs to be received?

   Who does Christ want to receive? What needs to happen first?

Stop for a moment and picture the door described in this passage. Christ is on the other side of this closed door. Be still, and listen for his voice. Wait in His presence. Is there anything you are having a hard time receiving from Him? Confess it to Him now, and ask Him to enable you to receive. Is there anything He is asking of you? Are you willing to open the door? Invite Him in, and spend some moments in His presence. What is He saying to you? Write out here what He is speaking to your heart.

4. In Acts 16, we find the story of one woman's conversion to Christ. How did Lydia's heart become open to the truth?

   When she became open to the truth, what else did she become open to?

   How has knowing Christ made you more open?

Telling the Truth

1. Read Psalms 51:1-6. In David's prayer, what does he say God desires?

   Telling the truth to ourselves about ourselves is not always easy. What does David say about himself?

   Stop right now and tell God the truth about yourself.

2. Read the following verses, and note what truth is accompanied by:

   Ephesians 4:15-16 _____

   John 1:14, 17 _____

   What does this tell us about how God views the truth about us?

   What does this tell us about how we are to speak the truth to ourselves and others?

   Does this give us the green light to tell the truth without thinking about consequences? How does compassion provide the necessary balance to truth-telling?

3. The truth is central to our Christian walk. List what each verse below reveals about the truth:

   John 14:6 _____

   John 15:26-27 _____

   John 8:32 _____

   Ephesians 4:25 _____

   II Timothy 2:23-25 _____

   I John 3:18-19 _____

In which of these areas do you personally have the hardest time with truth? Talk to God about it. Write one of these verses on an index card to carry with you, and meditate on throughout the day.

What is Love?

Our Love for God: In Psalms 18:1, David prays, "I love you, O Lord, my strength." The Hebrew word for *love* used in this passage means *to fondle, have compassion on, pity.* How intimate and surprising David's love for God is. Think for a moment what a difference it makes if we are compassionate toward God. Imagine how God feels when he is ignored or scorned by the ones He is calling to Himself. Stop right now and write a prayer to God, telling Him your thoughts and feelings on this. Then speak it out loud to Him.

God's Love for Us: Read Isaiah 63:9. Describe God's love for His people.

Who Are We to Love? (Matthew 5:43-4)

How Are We to Love? (Mark 12:28-31) (John 15:12)

Where Does this Love Come From? (Romans 5:1-5)

What Does It Mean to Love? Think of an example of the following types of love:

social or moral love (I John 3:11) _____

benevolent affection (I John 4:12) _____

brotherly fondness, kindness (I Peter 3:8)_____

Why is Love Essential? (I John 2:9-11, 4:16-17, 5:3)

Oliver Wendell Holmes once said, "Man's mind, once stretched by a new idea, never regains its original dimension." Allow your imagination to picture the Body functioning the way God intends, expressing all three kinds of love described above. Stay with the idea of God's idea of love flowing in and through the Body, long enough that your mind is stretched, and never regains any smaller dimension of understanding!

The Invitation

Read I John 3:11-24, and 4:20-21. Explain the life God is inviting us into.

Describe ways in which your life already looks like this.

Describe what you would like your future to look like, as you enter into this invitation to a life of love more fully.

4. Give examples of how you will show, or could show, all three kinds of love today.

How can we move into a lifestyle of living out all three types of love?

Close your eyes, and imagine that God has sent you an invitation, to this Life of Love, by special courier. Open it up. Notice what care He has taken, the lovely calligraphy, the beautiful paper. What does it say? Write your RSVP. Ask God to bring you opportunities to show all three kinds of love.

Relationship: The Priority

All of Scripture teaches that eternal life depends on a relationship with God, bearing fruit depends on a relationship with God, and that our relationships with others are a reflection of our relationship with God. Everything is about relationship. There is nothing more important. Relationship is *the key* to living a Fresh-Squeezed Life.

Yet **relationship is the most difficult challenge we face here on earth**. The most important relationships, with God and with family, are the most difficult of all. We want God and those we love to think like us, feel like us, and do what we want them to do. When that doesn't happen, we can easily become confused, angry, hurt, resentful and even feel betrayed.

We often don't even realize what our assumptions and expectations are until they are not met. Then we are surprised and blindsided by strong negative emotions, and we tend to blame the one who has disappointed us, instead of questioning our own assumptions and expectations.

When we attempt to build relationship within our spiritual family, we need to take a look at our assumptions and expectations going into it, because they will determine in part how we view what happens within those relationships. Assumptions in themselves are not bad. We all make many assumptions every day, and we don't even realize that we're making them most of the time. It's usually when they don't prove true that we can see them!

We have to make some basic assumptions just to function. Otherwise, we would spend all day doing tests on each chair before we sit in it, submitting our food to a lab for testing before we eat, climbing the stairs to the 8th floor because we don't assume the elevator will work.

We get into trouble by making assumptions *about God or about people*. If we assume that what seems right or logical or important or necessary *to us* is exactly what another person, or God, would think or say, or if we assume we know what another person feels based, for example, on a facial expression or a prayer request, we are going out on a limb that is sure to break underneath us at some point.

Even if we feel God is revealing something to us, we can jump to a wrong interpretation or conclusion, or deliver it with a critical or impatient attitude. I don't know why we think we are so good at figuring others out when we don't even know ourselves that well, but we often do.

Another way assumptions and expectations can get us into trouble is if we think others should always be at their best, always live perfectly according to Scriptural principles, never irritate us, never demand anything of us, and never have a bad day or a bad moment. Expecting perfection or even complete maturity from others will get us into trouble.

If instead we begin to cultivate an attitude of awe, respect and curiosity about the mystery of God, the mystery of another individual, knowing at once that we don't know much and yet wanting to know more, we can gradually develop relationships that are authentic, intimate and life changing.

I'm not talking here about the intellectual curiosity of a detached researcher or the always open ear that loves to hear a juicy bit of gossip. I'm talking about listening with heart, with openness, with anticipation that at any moment when we are with a friend, he or she will suddenly show us a truth about his or her soul; when we are praying or reading God's Word, suddenly we feel God's heart. What a moment!

If we are listening with heart, we will get ideas about how we can be a blessing to that person. Love has the impulse to give, to serve, to be generous with our time and resources.

If we are listening with heart, we recognize such sharing as a gift, a sacred trust. We receive it with warmth and compassion, even if it's not what we expected. This acceptance, given and received, allows us to venture deeper into the arena of relationship with this person, because it creates an atmosphere of emotional safety.

Acceptance is not the same as agreement or approval. It is far from easy, but it is a beautiful, reassuring, healing act. It takes us another step along the path to authentic intimate relationship. Why should we bother to try something difficult and complicated? Because **with God, it's all about relationship. It's top priority. And acceptance is the gateway**. Romans 15:7 tells us to accept each other as Christ has accepted us.

Let's learn to truly listen, to each other and to God, to see each other, and God, as mysteries to be revealed by littles, gems available for discovery, but not without looking and persisting, not without valuing what we've found when it finally appears. Some of the most wonderful words that can ever be spoken to another are, "Tell me more about that."

One of the most precious gifts we can ever hope to give is to listen with heart for, and receive with honor, the shining bits of truth offered up to us by a trusting soul.

One of the most precious gifts we can ever receive is to catch a glimpse of another's soul. Whether it's shared with tears, with laughter, anger, judgment or even sarcasm, we have been let in on a secret, the unfolding of another's self. What we do with it matters.

Knowing God

1. "Relationship is the key to the 'fresh-squeezed Life." Do you believe this statement is true? Explain.

2. Read John 17:1-3. Here Jesus says that having eternal life is knowing God and His Son. The word used here for "know" means to know absolutely, or to feel, be aware of, perceive and understand. How is this different from just believing that Jesus is the Son of God?

3. How can we actually know God and have a relationship with Him?

4. How satisfied are you with your experience in knowing/believing in God?

Spend some time with God, praying His Word to express the longing of your heart to know Him. (Some scriptures to pray: Psalms 13; Psalms 15; Psalms 16, Psalms 17; Psalms 18; Job 23:1-10; Psalms 25:1-5; Isaiah 26:3-9; Isaiah 33:2; Isaiah 64:1-9) Write below the verses that especially stir your heart as you pray:

Dwelling in Christ

Read John 15:1-8.

1. What proves you are a disciple of Christ?

2. What brings the Father glory?

3. What is the result of being attached to the Vine, being connected in relationship to Him?

4. What causes a branch to be thrown away?

5. Jesus says, "Remain in me and I will remain in you" (v. 4). The word for "remain" means "to stay in a given state or relation; dwell, continue, be present, wait for." What do you think this means?

6. How does it happen; what causes it? Do we have any control over it?

7. Read John 14:15 and and Matthew 22:37-39. What is the evidence that we love God?

What Does Love Look Like?

Read John 13:34-35.

1. What is it that can now happen in our relationships with others, simply because Jesus loves us, and we have experienced His love?

2. What effect will this have on unbelievers?

3. It is often said that "Words are cheap." James seems to agree. It is actions that tell the true story of someone's heart. What is his description of how a Christ-follower treats others? (See James 1:27; 2:1-4,8-9 15-16; 3:17-18; 4:1-2, 11-12.)

4. What does Love look like? Look up the following references, and write a word for each one that describes what is in Christ's heart as he encounters others:

Mt. 9:36 _____ Mt. 14:14 _____

Mt. 15:32 _____ Mt. 20:34 _____

Mk. 1:41 _____ Mk. 5:19 _____

Mk. 6:34 _____ Mk. 8:2 _____

5. When Christ feels compassion, what happens next?

6. When Jesus was preparing his disciples for his death, he told them, "Anyone who has faith in me will do what I have been doing" (from John 14:12). What had Jesus been doing?

But I Can't Do This!

Have you been reading these scriptures, and thinking to yourself, "I am so far from this! I can't do this!"? Let's see if we can extract some spiritual principles that will help us to figure out how all this happens.

1. Read Luke 6:38. Put into your own words the way you learn to live a life of compassion and giving toward others.

2. Read Luke 10:25-37. How would you describe the principle of relating to others Jesus is teaching?

3. Read Luke 10:38-42. Look for two important principles here. What can we learn from this short story?

4. Read Ephesians 2:21-22. Who is doing the building?

   What holds it together?

   What is the purpose of this building?

5. Jesus said, "I chose you and appointed you to go and bear fruit--fruit that will last...This is my command: Love each other" (from John 15:16-17). What is the principle of a life of love that Jesus has issued to all his followers? (Hint: Is it optional?)

   Does the fruit we are appointed to bear have anything to do with the command to love?

   Where does this fruit come from? Can we produce it on our own?

Admit your insufficiency to God, and ask Him to supernaturally connect and equip you.

Becoming the Body

1. Do you believe it is possible to fully accept someone without approving of them? Why or why not?

2. Do you believe it is possible to have unity with people who disagree with you? Why or why not?

3. Is it possible to disagree in a way that maintains friendship and love? What would that look like?

4. How does Jesus most often interact with people? (Look in Matthew, Mark, Luke or John, if you're not sure.) Do they have to ascribe to a certain doctrine before he accepts them or ministers to them?

5. Read Ephesians 4:1-16. What does unity in the Body of Christ look like? Describe the kind of church Paul is urging us to be.

6. In the above passage, Paul says that when we reach a state of unity, we will no longer be _____. The attainment of unity in the body is, therefore, a measure of our _____. "The whole body grows and builds itself up in love, as each part does its work" (from verse 16). Read this verse in your Bible; where does this unity and growth and effectiveness and love come from? _____. As we grow up, we grow into _____ (verse 15). So we grow from _____ and into _____, and in the process we become _____, "attaining to the whole measure of the fullness of Christ" (verse 13). Are we all capable of this? (see verse 7)

7. List the character traits God is calling us to, in an effort to "keep the unity"(see verses 2-3, 15-16):

Learning to Listen

1. Read Philippians 2:1-11. Explain how this passage shows us how to be better listeners by becoming more like Christ.

2. How does Colossians 2:18-19 describe someone who does not listen, and wants everyone to listen to him?

3. Our world often describes its values with sayings, such as "It's a dog-eat-dog world," or "May the best man win," but God's kingdom operates differently. How are we to treat the timid and the weak? (See I Thessalonians 5:14)

   What can we specifically do to obey this scripture?

4. How are we to treat the poor? (See James 2:1-5)

5. How does a person with spiritual wisdom and understanding live? (James 3:17-18)

   Do you think this person is a good listener?
   Explain.

6. If we discern something negative in another, such as being judgmental or irritable or manipulative, how can we use this information to transform this moment into something positive? How can we avoid judging and being irritable in return, and instead make it count for Christ's kingdom?

James 1:19, 26 says: "Take note of this: Everyone should be quick to listen, slow to speak and slow to become angry...If anyone considers himself religious and yet does not keep a tight rein on his tongue, he deceives himself and his religion is worthless."

Stop and take inventory right now; ask God to help you in areas where you need to grow.

Restoration and Transformation: The Purpose

God is in the business of restoration and transformation. It is His heart to restore and transform. His hand is always open, His eyes are always searching for an opportunity to perform his pleasure: relationship with his people; relationship with God *always* results in transformation and restoration. He has created us all, and Christ died for all. He desires for *all* people to experience relationship with Him, and transformation by Him.

Mark 1:21-27 relates an event that occurs soon after Jesus calls the twelve disciples to follow Him. He delivers a man from an evil spirit. The people are amazed, and ask, "What new doctrine is this?" They recognize that *their understanding of the intent and purpose of God is being transformed* right before their eyes; this is a *new* doctrine to them.

Not only that, but *the life of the man is instantly transformed*. Now instead of crying out against Jesus, he is free to praise Him. His former sanity and free will are restored to him by an authoritative word from the Christ. As soon as Jesus begins his earthly ministry, he sets about transforming and restoring.

Suddenly everything is new, transformed, or about to be: new wine, new wineskins, a new covenant between God and man, a new commandment, new doctrine, a new Passover Lamb, a new creation, a new and living way, new heavens, new earth, a new name, the new Jerusalem, a new song. Just to make sure we get it, that God is in the business of transforming things and making them new, John records in his vision of heaven, "He who was seated on the throne said, 'I am making everything new'" (Revelation 21:5). God is transforming *everything*!

This has always been His heart and His purpose; **when Christ came, He revealed to us *the extent* of God's *will* to restore and transform**. **He revealed *the depth* of God's yearning *heart* to restore and transform.** In order to redeem us from sin, to restore us to right relationship with Him, Christ was willing to live on earth as a human being, to take our sins upon Himself and to die in our stead. And the Father was willing to let Him. That's how much God wants to restore to us what we lost in the Fall.

If this is God's work, it is also our work here on earth. Once we accept His invitation to relationship with Him, He begins His work of restoring and transforming us from the inside out. It is never done, as long as we are living on this earth. We are not just passive recipients of this transformative, restorative work, though. We are called to a life of active self-denial and self-control in cooperation with God's Spirit, so that we may be "conformed to the image of Christ."

Not only that, we are to live out and give out this same invitation to others: that they too might be transformed by the living God, and experience His restorative power in their lives. We do that by reflecting, radiating, and pouring out God's essential nature, which is Love, and by telling others Who Love is.

We are to cooperate with God in the restoration of what Satan has stolen: it starts with salvation, but it doesn't end there. God wants to restore first relationship with God, then everything else: pure-hearted relationship with each other, health, blessing, joy, peace, purpose, freedom, spiritual passion. God knows how to give good gifts to His children. Everything good comes from above. Why? Because it is who God is, and so it is what He does.

In the same way, James tells us, words are cheap; you are not who you *say* you are; you are what you *do*. Who are you?

We are to be God's representatives on this earth! Think of it! Jesus said, They will know you belong to Me, *because of your love for one another*. We begin loving within the family, but immediately it shows and overflows, and touches those around us. The family of God was never meant to be a closed system. We were never meant to sit around waiting to figure out God's will before we do anything. We were never told to get perfected first, and then reach out to others. **The work of restoration always begins now**.

Even in the Old Testament, before the empowerment of the Holy Spirit actually taking up residence within us, God expected His people to get busy doing His will. "Don't drag your feet! God has chosen you to take your place before Him to serve; this is your life work; make sure you do it and do it well" (II Chronicles 29:11, THE MESSAGE translation).

How do we do this work and do it well? *Love.*

Love is *costly*. It will take some time to show love. It might even take a little money. It might even require us to give up our reputation, our dignity, our membership in a group or club. It will require patience, and other fruit of the Spirit. We will definitely have to pray, because the kind of love that draws others to Christ comes from Him; the only way to have it flowing through us is to be fully connected to Him. Love will definitely cost us.

Love is *open-hearted*; *it both gives and receives.* It wants to know, to listen, to extend itself in acceptance of "what is" and wait expectantly for the better thing that is to come. This love is humble enough to be dependent on its source; it only springs out of relationship with God. It wants to give, and is comfortable with both giving and receiving.

Love is *accountable* to God, His Word, and His people. It confesses its own faults, forgives the faults of others, and, instead of wasting energy judging and resenting others, it yearns to see Christ formed in others, to see full restoration of what they've lost.

Love is *truthful*. It does not think of itself more highly than it ought, but sees clearly and humbly. It wants to know the truth and to speak the truth, and to speak it only in love, first of all to ourselves about ourselves.

This loving heart comes to each new day with its sleeves rolled up. Yes, it first sits at the feet of Jesus and learns from Him and adores Him, as Mary did; this is choosing the best and putting God first. Then it gets busy. The problem with Martha was not that she worked. The problem was that she thought it was all up to her. She thought serving others was about her strength and talents. Instead of first becoming centered in and filled with Jesus, she sprang into action. She became exhausted, and then resentful because she was doing it all, and it felt like too much. She probably thought she didn't have a choice, but she did. So do we. This way of love is to have a heart that is open to *both* God and others. "Whatever you did for one of the least of these brothers of mine, you did for me," Jesus says (Matthew 25:40). So let's serve others, and learn to do it gracefully, not with a "poor me" mentality.

We are to comfort others "in any trouble with the comfort we ourselves have received from God" (II Corinthians 1:4). Have you received God's comfort? Then you have it to give. Keep your heart open and tender toward others in their distress, rather than believing that you have had it worse than them, or that you should be the one receiving comfort. Widen your hearts!

He takes pity on us as dust (Psalms 103:13-14); therefore, we also take pity on others, realizing their need for the comfort and compassion of God expresses through His people.

It is His kindness that moves us to repentance (Romans 2:4), and it will be our kindness toward others that draws them to Him. Here's the thing: Life is really tough sometimes. It can be lonely and scary and confusing. People can be cruel and harsh and demanding and indifferent. We are *all* the walking wounded. No one person has a corner on misery.

The truth is that we all yearn for the same things: To be seen, to be heard, to be accepted, to be loved, to be valued for who we are and what we bring to the table, to be appreciated, to be forgiven, to be of some use in this world. We all want to know that we are both lovable and capable.

We all need these things. Many of us did not get these things in our families of origin. All of us learned relationship imperfectly. We go on to attempt relationship imperfectly throughout our lives. We wound others and get wounded.

God wants to get in there and restore to us what we lost or never had. He wants to transform our hearts toward Him and toward others. As we take the risk of entering into true relationship with God, our relationship wounds can be healed. We experience with God first-hand the exquisite tenderness of a loving Father's reassurance or rebuke. It is all so bathed in gentleness and love that we can receive it all, the comfort and the correction, because with it is only acceptance and kindness and grace.

There is no rejection or harshness. With God there is no list He keeps of our wrongs that He reminds us of when we flub up yet again. As we are in relationship with our Heavenly Father, we experience true Love. As we receive, so then we are able to give.

We have received from God patience, acceptance, love, forgiveness, gentleness. We are valued just as we are. We are valued for who we are to Him in Christ. And we are valued for the unique gifts and talents He has created in us.

He never gives up on us. He lets us cry and scream and throw our tantrums and then He lets us crawl back into His lap and be held. We know that He knows us fully and still loves us forever.

This is our model for loving others. Do we say we love, yet criticize, judge and reject? Do we speak to or about others in patronizing or condescending terms, assuming we know more or are qualified to judge them as lacking in some way? When someone confesses a struggle or requests prayer, do we imply they must be lacking in faith? Then our proclamations of love mean little; our actions tell the truth.

If only always when we look at each other, we remember to see that each one of us is created to be a temple for the living God, that just as the Holy of Holies in Solomon's temple was overlaid with gold, so God intends to overlay the innermost being of that one and that one and that one with purest gold. He intends to overlay *your* innermost being with gold; you are that precious to Him.

I need to value you, because our Father values you as an exquisite treasure. He is tenderly, patiently, endlessly at work in you, drawing you to Himself, building on the dustof your past griefs and losses and wounds a Holy Place where He will meet you and love you and transform you.

I want to cooperate with God in this. It is not my job to change you or control you. It is my job to love you. And it is your job to love me. **Part of loving each other is realizing that we will both do this very imperfectly. We need grace from each other.** I will try to be responsive to you rather than reactive, and you will try, too; but I need to realize that if I tramp around and stomp on your emotional toes, I can expect you to say *ouch* and say it loudly! Then we'll need to forgive each other, truly forgive, and move on.

Relationship: it's all about relationship: relationship with God and relationship with people. All the Law and the prophets are summed up in two commands: Love God. Love others.

We will fail at this. We will fail again and again. We have failed in the past and we know it, and we know we will continue to fail in the present and in the future. Pray this prayer for His Body each day this week:

Oh, God, give us courage to continue to enter into relationship, to fall on You in repentance when we fail, and be broken again and again. Give us the sweetness of heart toward You to not allow a root of bitterness to spring up, but rather to let our brokenness be the soft soil in which we learn to grow Love. Transform us, O God! Amen.

"And we who with unveiled faces all reflect the Lord's glory are being transformed into His likeness with every-increasing glory, which comes from the Lord who is the Spirit." (II Corinthians 3:18)

Restoration

1. Read Luke 5:1-10. What did Jesus call Simon Peter to do?

2. Read the following passages:

    Luke 5:12-13   Matthew 8:1-3   Matthew 8:5-7   Matthew 8:16

    What did the people have to do in order to receive a blessing from Christ?

3. What does this mean for us today; how are we to look at ministry, within the church and outside the church?

4. Read Luke 5:17-26. Explain how Jesus seems to view meeting people's physical and spiritual needs.

5. God has revealed His heart's desire to restore what we lost in the Fall. List here everything you can think of that we lost when sin entered:

6. List here which of these God has already restored to you:

7. What have you lost in childhood?

    In failed relationships?

    As a result of bad choices?

    As a result of someone else's bad choices?

Ask God now to restore to you what still needs to be restored.

Transformation

1. What do you think brings about the transformation of lives?

2. Tell a "before and after" transformation story about something in your life that has changed.

3. Read II Corinthians 5:16-21 or Ephesians 2:4-9. Put this "before and after" story into a single sentence.

4. Accepting Christ brings transformation, but the work of transformation continues throughout our Christian lives. Read Romans 6:11-14. Explain in your own words one of the ways transformation takes place.

5. Romans 5:3-5 tells another way transformation occurs in our lives. Put this into your own words, as if you were explaining it to a friend, then add a personal example from your own life.

6. II Corinthians 3:17-18 shows that transformation comes from seeing _____ _____.

7. Read Galatians 5:16-25. Transformation occurs with _____.

8. In John 15:3, II Timothy 3:16-17, and Hebrews 4:12-13, we see that _____ _____ transforms us. From these verses, list the ways it changes us:

Our Part in Restoration and Transformation

1. If God wants to bring restoration in your life, how do you think He feels about restoration in the lives of others?

2. What role do you believe He wants you to play in inviting others to experience restoration? Be specific.

3. Read Isaiah 48:17-18. What does God want to restore to His people?

   What is our part in the restoration process?

4. 4. God doesn't just restore what has been damaged or lost; He actually transforms! List what He transforms, and what part we play in the transformation process:

   Romans 12:2 God transforms_____, and we_____.

   II Corinthians 11:15 God transforms_____, and we_____.

   Isaiah 45:9 God transforms_____, and we_____.

   Ephesians 2:10 God transforms_____, and we_____.

   Ephesians 3:7-9 God transformed_____, and he_____.

   Ephesians 4:22-24 God transforms_____, and we_____.

   Proverbs 3:5-6 God transforms_____as we_____.

   Proverbs 2:1-5 God transforms_____when we_____.

   II Corinthians 5:17 God transforms_____when we_____.

   Hebrews 10:19-22 God has transformed_____and we_____.

   Hebrews 9:11-14 God transforms_____ and we_____.

5. On our own we fall short of _____ (Romans 3:23), but we now have the power to choose to do all _____ (I Corinthians 10:31).

Wow. That's transformation!

Our Transformation Into the Body of Christ

1. Read Ephesians 2:21-22 and I Peter 2:5-10. The Body of Christ is like a _____, built with _____ stones. Explain some ways this illustration makes sense to you.

2. What do you think it means for us to be a "holy priesthood?"

3. Read Ephesians 4:15-16. Here the Body of Christ is described as a _____ _____.

4. In Colossians 1:10-12, the Body of Christ is described as _____ _____. Which of the above illustrations appeals to you the most? _____ Why?

5. How does this transformation from many separate individuals into the functioning Body of Christ occur?

Our Transformation Within the Body of Christ

God has a lot to say about how the Body of Christ is intended to function. Read the following passages and write down the character traits God wants from us.

1. Ephesians 4:25-5:21:

2. Philippians 2:1-11:

3. Colossians 3:11-17:

4. Hebrews 13:1:

5. I Peter 3:8-9:

6. I Peter 4:8-11:

Ask God to show you how you are doing in these areas. Wait in His presence expectantly. As you realize what He is saying to you, you may want to write it down so you can continue this dialogue with God about becoming part of His Body. Ask Him for His empowerment and guidance to be obedient in this area.

Transformation of the Body

As each member of the Body grows in grace and knowledge, this individual transformation has an effect on the Body as a whole. When we function correctly as the Body of Christ, what happens? How do we affect the lives of others, both inside and outside the Body?

1. Hebrews 10:24-25:

2. James 2-4:

3. James 5:13-16:

4. James 5:19-20:

5. If you had to describe what the Body looks like, what its essential quality is, in only one word, or one phrase, what would it be?

    Why did you choose this word (phrase)?

6. What will be the result of the Body functioning like this, according to the will and plan of God?

Giving Out the River: The Plan

"'Whoever believes in me, as the Scripture has said, streams of living water will flow from within him.' By this he meant the Spirit" (John 7:38-39). The plan is for us to give out the river, to let the Spirit of God flow from us out to others.

The plan is for us to choose "the most excellent way" of Love (I Corinthians 13). Nothing great or impressive that we do or accomplish means anything without Love, God's Love, God's Spirit, flowing through us.

This is the plan: patience, kindness, generosity of spirit, humility, courtesy, forgiveness, joy, truth, protectiveness, trust, hope, and perseverance in our dealings with each other.

"Follow the way of love" (I Corinthians 14:1). This is the life journey of choosing what is better: the way of intimate relationship with Christ lived out in demonstrated love toward others.

The better path that Mary chose was to sit at the feet of Jesus. It has always been God's invitation, from the beginning of recorded time, to live in relationship with Him, to be joyfully and reverently at His feet, moment by moment subservient and hungry and open, and then to serve others *from that experience of being infused with and empowered by His truth, His love, and His grace.*

David doesn't always get it right, but often he does. In Chapter 22 of I Chronicles, we see how much David's heart longs to see the Temple built. God has told him, "No, your son will build it." So David thinks and dreams and yearns for that day. He collects thousands of tons of gold and silver, as well as the other raw materials needed to build the Temple.

At the end of his life, he hands over the kingdom to his son Solomon and reveals God's plan that he, not David, will build the Temple. He lists the incredible bulk of materials gathered for this daunting project.

He tells the leaders of Israel, "Is not the Lord your God with you? And has he not granted you rest on every side? Now devote your heart and soul to *seeking the Lord your God.*" Whoa! If he were going by human wisdom, he would have said, "Now devote yourself heart and soul *to building this Temple.*"

How did David come to instruct the faithful in this way? He understood the principles of "giving out the river." Projects are great. Acting on God's promises is a good thing. Serving God and others is the goal. But *first things first*.

Building a temple is a good thing. Serving others is a great thing. Seeking God is the *best* thing. It's not either/or. We don't have to wait until we are spiritual giants to accomplish anything or serve others. David says, "Devote yourselves to seeking God. *Begin to build*." It's both/and: **Seek God *and* begin the work**. We tend to get it backward: devote yourself to the project, and ask God's blessing on it. This is a way that seems right but isn't. We are to acknowledge *as we are serving* that the Love we give comes only through His empowerment, and it continues to flow only as we stay connected in a Love relationship to Him; therefore we continually seek Him.

We don't develop Christlikeness by building temples, making sacrifices, tithing, feeding the poor or teaching Bible studies. We develop Christlikeness when we do these things as an outgrowth and expression of our relationship with Him. One thing is needful: Devote yourself to God. Then and only then will your work be infused with His Life, His Love. This is the "*better* way." This work will bear fruit. This work will bring others to Christ. "By this all men will know that you are my disciples, if you love one another" (John 13:35).

If we devote ourselves to God, and "have the mind of Christ," we will serve others; we will draw others to God. *This is what He is all about.* This way of seeking God first, and letting Him direct the river, may be *costly*. You may have to give up your own way, your own plans, your own priorities, your own logic, from time to time. David did.

This way of serving others is *open in giving and receiving*: David gave his time, expertise, experience for something he would not accomplish, see or get the credit for. He gave anyway. He received gifts from neighboring kings; he dedicated the plunder of war to the temple supplies; he freely received and put it where his heart was: in the temple treasuries.

David was *truthful* in his service. He admitted, he agreed with God, that he was a man of blood and therefore could not build the temple himself. He wasn't resentful or bitter about this. He got busy doing what he could do: collect what would be needed when the Temple was built after he was gone. What a heart for God's work!

David, even though he was king of Israel, was *accountable*; there were officials in charge of guarding and keeping record of all the treasure that had been dedicated and set aside for the temple.

David has inspired the people to seek God wholeheartedly, and to enter wholeheartedly into the work of building the Temple. There is another piece of this fresh-squeezed Life revealed in this story.

It is not enough to seek God and to serve Him. This sounds like plenty, but it's not. There is another essential requirement, and without this everything else eventually falls apart. Without this we turn into the Pharisees, whitewashed tombs that look great on the outside but inside are full of death, rottenness and stench.

David knows God's blessing and guidance depend on the people getting this important piece into their hearts, so he assembles the officials and the warriors. He addresses them with such warmth. "Listen to me, my brothers and my people" (I Chronicles 28:2). What a king! The common people are not common to him, but rather his family, his own people.

First he addresses them with love, then makes sure the transition of power to his son, a man of peace, goes smoothly. What a picture! I imagine this scene in my mind and see Love and Peace standing in unity shoulder to shoulder. What a reminder to let Love and Peace rule in our hearts and inform what we say and how we say it, what we do and how we do it. When we do this, there will be unity.

So far all has been sweetness and light, a positive message, easy to swallow. We love that, don't we? Here comes the thick slice of raw onion in the sandwich. It's good for you but it has a bite to it. Verse 8: *Be careful.*

David is delivering a warning. *Be careful to follow all the commands of the Lord your God, that you may possess this good land and pass it on as an inheritance.* The good life in a good land serving the Most High God is here; it's yours. *Be careful.*

Reading God's Word, worshiping with other believers, memorizing and teaching Scripture, even serving as a pastor or missionary, planting churches, supporting church building projects, giving to the poor...this beautiful life can come to a sad or violent or even shameful end if we don't pay attention here.

Be careful to follow all the commandments of the Lord. Your welfare and blessings depend on it and not just yours. Count on it: if your life goes down in flames, you will singe those closest to you.

Truly seeking God leads to humble obedience. We read His commands and we take them to heart. We bow in adoration and holy fear before the God who holds everything in His hands. This work is never over. There is always more growth that God wants to work in us. The closer we get to God, the more aware we are of His awesome power; the closer we get to God, the more we are aware of not just the kindness of God, but also the severity of God. Accepting His invitation to be adopted into His family comes with demands for us to truly be His children, not just *appear* to be His children.

David goes on to publicly give Solomon a charge in verses 9-10. Acknowledge God. Serve with devotion and a willing mind, for the Lord searches every heart and understands every motive. The Lord has chosen you. Be strong. Do the work.

Here David lets us know the secret of obedience: if our motive is to truly know, love and please God, if we serve Him wholeheartedly and willingly, we will most naturally, or rather supernaturally in the Spirit, learn to obey Him and reverence Him.

This obedience part of having a relationship with God was the hardest part for David and it is the hardest part for many of us. It took him a lifetime to get it right. David speaks out of his own remembered heartaches, the times his own disobedience brought horrific consequences. I can almost see the intensity in his gaze, the tears in his eyes, the firm grip as he clutches his son's hand, imploring him to be wiser, more obedient, than his father.

His message to the new king is straightforward. Seek God. *Be careful.* Obey God. The good life is within your grasp. *Be careful.* If you disobey, you could lose it all. *Be careful.* Be strong. Do the work. *Be careful.*

Disobedience to God's commands always hurts us and always, always hurts others. All the efforts we make to serve others and encourage relationships are wasted if we damage those relationships by our disobedience to God.

Obedience is necessary to, and proof of, our love for God. "If you obey my commands," Jesus told his disciples, " you will remain in my love" (John 15:10). How do we know his commands? There is no other way than devoting time and effort to our relationship with God, spending time in prayer and spending time in the Word, and then *taking what we hear and read to heart.* **We have to know Him to obey Him**. Going to church all by itself just won't do it. God does not accept our tears and "I love you's" if we then spend our lives gratifying ourselves, and never have the time or heart to know Him, please Him and serve Him.

"Remain in me, and I will remain in you" (John 15:4).

"As the Father has loved me, so have I loved you. Now remain in my love. If you obey my commands, you will remain in my love. I have told you this so that my joy may be in you and that your joy may be complete. My command is this: Love each other as I have loved you. Greater love has no one than this, that he lay down his life for his friends. This is my command: Love each other" (from John 15:9-17).

What is the work to which God has called you? What exactly is His plan? "Love each other." How can you do this work? Obey Him; remain in His presence and His Word.

If we are loving and serving in His strength, he says that His *joy* will be in us.

What a Life! Seek God, *and* begin to build.

Give out the River!

Staying in the River's Path

1. Read Luke 10:38-42. Reflect for a moment on your own daily life. When are you most distracted, overworked, and likely to feel resentment toward others?

   Adopt the practice of meditating on a variation of verses 41-42, repeating it over and over again to yourself, when you find yourself becoming irritable or exhausted:

   "_____, _____, you are worried and upset about many things, but
          (your own name)
   only one thing is needed. Choose what is better, and it will not be taken away from you."

2. When do you routinely make time for reading the Word and prayer? (If you don't already do this, make this commitment to yourself now.)

3. Psalms 119 is a window into the heart of someone who deeply desires to know and live out God's Word. Read the entire Psalms aloud to God as a prayer. Now, using the verses that best express your heart at this moment, create your own psalm to God about His Word, and write it down here. Just as Psalms 119 opens up the heart of the psalmist, God's Word opens up His heart to us. Don't you long to be more in tune with His heart?

Yielding to the River

1. Read II Samuel 7:1-13. As soon as David settles in as King, what is in his heart to do?

2. The Word of God comes to him through the prophet Nathan, and says, in effect: *I am going to do all kinds of great things for you, and you will do all kinds of great things for Me; but the one thing that is in your heart to do, I will not allow you to do.* Now read II Samuel 7:18-22. How does David respond to this disappointing news?

3. In these passages from II Samuel, which phrases particularly impress you, and show you the attitude of David's heart?

4. Read Psalms 12:6. Write a list of words that describe David's attitude toward the Word of God.

5. Read Psalms 19:7-8. Here we find a list of words that describe God's Word, each one followed by a result or work of God's Word in our lives. Write these here:

    The Word of God is _____, and it _____.

    The Word of God is _____, and it _____.

    The Word of God is _____, and it _____.

    The Word of God is _____, and it _____.

6. Now the pattern is altered. Instead of the Word of the Lord, suddenly David describes the *fear* of the Lord (verse 9). What do you believe the reason for that is?

7. Verses 9-11 further describe the Word of God, and list another important function in our lives. What is it?

8. Read I Chronicles 22:1-14. Immediately after David's experience with God on the threshing floor, he knows that this is the future site of the Temple. He begins preparations for the Temple, even though he knows he won't get to build it himself. Taking all these passages into consideration, why do you believe David is able to accept wholeheartedly God's will, even though it is the opposite of what he himself wants?

Pouring Out the River

In I Chronicles 22:19, David instructs his people, "Now devote your heart and soul to seeking the Lord your God. Begin to build..."

This is what God always says to His people: *Devote your heart and soul to seeking Me. Begin to build for My kingdom.*

This is what He said to David; however, David's part in the building was not *construction* of the Temple. His part was to plan, envision, and lay up treasures in *preparation* for its construction.

Let this be your meditation throughout this week:

"Now devote your heart and soul to seeking the Lord your God. Begin to build."

Ask God to make it plain to you what your unique part is; how does He want you to be involved in building His kingdom?

Seek Him heart and soul, and ask for revelation and insight. Keep asking. As you hear from God, jot down here what He is telling you about how you are to build. What are you drawn to? What area of service do you long for?

Measuring Success: Flowing With the River

For any project, success is measured by the degree to which the original goal is met. When we are building for the kingdom of God, God is the One and Only "City Planner." He is the only One capable of judging our work.

"Each one should be careful how he builds. For no one can lay any foundation other than the one already laid which is Jesus Christ. If any man builds on this foundation using gold, silver, costly stones, wood, hay or straw, his work will be shown for what it is, because the Day will bring it to light. It will be revealed with fire, and the fire will test the quality of each man's work. If what he has built survives, he will receive his reward. If it is burned up, he will suffer loss" (from I Corinthians 3:10-15).

How do you think we can be careful how we build? What do you think Paul is trying to say? (Refer to the context, I Corinthians 3:1-9.)

In what other ways can we be careful how we build? (For insight, you may want to read II Timothy 3:16-17, Romans 9:20-21, Romans 9:30-32, Romans 12:1-2, Romans 12:4-8, Romans 13:9-10.)

Staying In His Will: Becoming One With the River

1. God's will is for us to _____ (John 15:17).

2. Read John 15:9-17. Jesus gave his *physical* human life for us to redeem us back to the Father, but here He is not saying that this is the greatest human love. Rather, he says, "Greater love has no one than this, that he lay down his *ego* for his friends. This is my command: Love each other."

   He seems to be saying that the key to loving is to sacrifice our egos for each other. What do you think that means?

3. Think of three specific examples of someone sacrificing his own ego for the good of another.
   a.

   b.

   c.

4. I Peter 3:8-9 exhorts us to "live in harmony with one another; be sympathetic, love as brothers, be compassionate and humble. Do not repay evil with evil or insult with insult, but with blessing, because to this you were called so that you may inherit a blessing."

   How does being compassionate keep us from disobedience?

   How does it build up the Body?

   How does it further God's kingdom, conquering darkness with light?

Kingdom Forces On the Move!

When we submit to God's right to rule, when we learn to trust His heart toward us, joy can flood into our souls right in the middle of disaster. David prayed, "I am radiant with joy because of your mercy, for you have listened to my troubles and have seen the crisis in my soul" (Psalms 31:7). Mother Teresa said, "Joy is a net of love by which you can catch souls." How are you *this week* moving into joy and advancing God's kingdom?

Consecration: Our Treasures in God's Treasuries

Continuing to follow this story of the kingdom's transfer of power from David to Solomon, in I Chronicles 29 David tells the whole assembly of Israel how much wealth he has already dedicated to the building of the Temple. In verse 3, he goes a step further: "Besides all this, in my devotion to the temple of my God, I now give my personal treasures."

What an example to his people! He is demonstrating that love for God, this Life of walking with God, is *costly*; it *requires giving as well as receiving*; everyone, even the most wealthy, powerful individual in the land, is *accountable*; and it *requires truth-telling*.

David has amassed for the building of the Temple an almost unimaginable storehouse of riches. He could have stopped right there and said, "It is sufficient." Interestingly enough, he doesn't do that. He immediately issues a personal challenge to everyone standing there. "Now who is willing to consecrate himself to the Lord?"

Their walk with God, their devotion to God, is just as important as his. He can't do it for them. **There are outward signs, but the work is inward**, and each person must "work out his own salvation" (Philippians 2:12).

All the leaders responded freely and wholeheartedly to the call. They said yes to consecration. **The word consecration means to set apart, devote, separate**. They weren't asked to consecrate their precious stones and precious metals. **The call was to consecrate *themselves*.** When they did that, they felt more attached to God than they did to their things. When they separated themselves *for* God, suddenly they were able to separate *from* their wealth, and they wanted it to go toward the Temple.

David could have said, "No, don't go that far, there's no need, we already have so much." He didn't. He let them give. They needed this. Their necessary spiritual walk with God required the same things as David's did, and he was wise not to deprive them of it.

This devotion to God was for them:

69

costly,

active in willing, cheerful giving,

accountable, and

truthful; that is, expressing the true motives of their hearts.

David didn't require it; he allowed it.

He modeled it.

He inspired it.

He invited it.

He rejoiced in it.

David and Israel's leaders could be feeling pretty proud of themselves right about now, confident in their ability to move forward. Instead, out of David's mouth and heart comes a very different attitude: "But who am I, and who are my people that we should be able to give? **Everything comes from you, and we have given you only what comes from your hand**."

Such humility. Such gratitude. The outpouring of a grateful, humble soul is a thing of beauty to the heart of God. At that moment, a creature is in harmony with his Creator, and all is as it should be.

In David's prayer we hear reverence and spiritual wisdom. He is giving to God because God first gave to him. He can see the giving/receiving exchange of the relationship clearly. He sees that this relationship is costing him, yet he gives joyfully, gratefully, willingly, humbly.

He knows it has cost God far more in grief to watch His children rebel and disobey and flounder in their faith. They have come to this moment only because of the love and grace of God. David clearly gets now that integrity, the truthful, accountable piece of relationship, is of top importance to God (verse 17).

It's not the outward show God cares about; it's the inward intent. That's what matters in our earthly relationships, as well.

As David sees all of this, his heart is softened completely with gratitude and humility. God doesn't have to love His people, but He does. David sees that everything, not just material wealth but every good thing, is a divine gift. When we have this attitude, we can hold onto our material blessings lightly. We appreciate our non-material blessings, not as our due, but as a sweet gift from our heavenly Father.

The **humble, grateful heart is another essential piece of this Love thing, this fresh-squeezed Life with God and others.** If we measure our love for others or God only by the yardstick of costly-accountable-reciprocal-truthful-obedient, if we can check all those off, we might feel pretty superior. At that moment of feeling that we are getting an A+, perhaps qualified to judge others, and those around us had better just appreciate it, we have lost it. We are no longer in a humble, grateful attitude, and our "love" will come across as judgmental, withholding, resentful, and superior.

Instead, if in this love we are holding someone accountable, it is with complete humility. "If you think you are standing firm, be careful that you don't fall!" (I Corinthians 10:12). If we are telling the truth as we see it, we will be careful that we are "speaking the truth in love" (Ephesians 4:15). If we are not receiving what we want from God or another person, we are still able, in love, to see and be grateful for the good things that have come our way.

If a relationship has been costly, ideally the cost will have been matched and measured by love. If, over time, the giving/receiving in a human relationship is seriously out of balance, we may have a decision to make about whether it should be allowed to continue as it is, but the decision will be made, delivered and carried out with an attitude of grace, intending to inflict no harm and desiring the best for that person.

If there have been intentional offenses committed against us by another person, we may speak out of our anger and hurt, and then be grieved in our spirits that we did not handle things better. This is not the end of the story. It will take time for us to arrive completely at this place of heartfelt forgiveness, but we can and must make the decision to forgive now. We need to extend to ourselves the same grace we have learned to extend to other hurting souls. *If we are seeking God first*, we will eventually get there.

Humble gratitude is a grace beyond valuing. It is the essence and foundation of the loving heart. It is a key to the joyful fresh-squeezed Life.

The way of Life, the "most excellent way" of Love, is:

costly,
accountable,
reciprocal,
truthful,
obedient to God, *and*
humbly grateful.

Just as David became more godly the longer he kept loving, seeking and spending time with God, so will we. As we become more godly, the people with whom we are in relationship will be inspired and invited to go deeper in their walk with God, too. Our humble, grateful hearts will want to give out the River; our humble grateful hearts will want to give what God has asked and more, and then more. Our treasures in God's treasuries. What a privilege.

Personal Consecration

1. How are you as a believer "set apart" from the world?

   From your former life?

2. How do you "set apart" time for Bible reading and study?

   Is there a routine or ritual or reminder that you build into your day to help you make that consecration? If so, what is it?

   What is the place you routinely use for this?

   How do you make it easy to do your reading and studying? (For example, do you have all your study helps in one place?)

3. How do you consecrate time for prayer and worship?

   What draws you to, or reminds you of, this commitment?

4. Do you have regular time set apart for serving others? What are they?

5. When you have a particular task to accomplish, do you pray or ask for prayer to be set apart by God for guidance and empowerment?

6. David asked, "Now who is *willing...*?" Do you instead feel burdened by these opportunities for personal consecration, and guilty when you have fallen short, more than you feel cheerful and willing? If so, how do you handle that?

Set a goal for yourself in the area of personal consecration. What is next in your faith journey? Discuss this with the Lord. Wait silently for Him to speak.

Perspective on Life

1. Psalms 34:8 says, "Oh, taste and see that the Lord is good!" How has your view of God changed, now that you know Him?

   Following Christ results in a radical change in our view on many things. How has being a Christ-follower given you a different perspective on yourself?

   On others?

2. Do you believe Christ-followers have a new perspective on serving the needs of others? If so, how?

   On spending money? Explain.

3. Psalms 36:9 says, "In your light, we see light." Explain one opinion or belief that you have radically changed since becoming a believer.

   Why did you make this change?

4. Read Isaiah 40:25-31. This passage is one of many that describes a change in viewpoint. Here God is telling his people to get a new perspective on life, one that acknowledges His greatness and His involvement in their lives. Read verse 31 again. The eagle's perspective is far different from that of an ant. What leads to our being able to have the eagle's perspective?

5. Read Ephesians 2:1-10. Here Paul spells out some before-and-after-truths. List these opposites:

Before accepting Christ	_After accepting Christ_
dead in sins (v.1)	alive with Christ (v.4)

Perspective on Treasures

Read Matthew 6:19-21. Here Jesus exhorts his followers to adopt a life-changing perspective on every aspect of daily life. Your perspective is "how you see things." Jesus uses the metaphor of the eye to make the concept of perspective easy for us to understand.

1. In verse 22, Jesus says, "The eye is the lamp of the body. If your eyes are good, your whole body will be full of light." For a moment, re-read this verse and substitute the words "your perspective" for the words "the eye" and "your eyes." What word would you then use instead of "body?" Read verses 22-23 with this in mind.

   What do you think Jesus is trying to get across to us?

2. In verses 19-20, Jesus tells us to "store up treasures in heaven." What do you think He means by this? What are some different ways we can store up treasures in heaven?

3. Verse 21 says that "where our treasure is, there our hearts will be also." What does this mean?

4. Jesus continues to talk about the things money can buy in verses 25-34. Read this passage. In verses 31-34, he explains the radical change in perspective we have when we realize that our God cares about our needs and also has the power to meet them. The world is on a treadmill running to acquire more and more things, more and more treasure on earth. Christ exhorts his followers to seek first and foremost _____.

   How true is this of you?

5. Read Malachi 3:6-18. Here God has a serious complaint about His people. What is it?

6. What is the result of their sin?

7. Verses 16-18 reveal what God's treasure is: _____
   _____

Perspective on Spiritual Principles

We tend to go to one extreme or another: either legalism (proving we are "spiritual" by doing all the "right" things) or lazy grace (assuming that because "God is Love," we don't have to hold ourselves accountable to follow any rules at all)!

When we get serious about following Jesus, we find He doesn't play games! He wants *all* of us; He wants us to obey, serve and give joyfully out of our genuine love for Him.

1. Read Matthew 23:23. Explain Christ's attitude toward tithing, that is, the practice of giving 1/10 of one's income to the church.

2. How does this verse relate to Matthew 6:19-21?

3. Explain how Matthew 23:23 relates to Ephesians 2:10:

4. Read II Corinthians 8:7-12. What were the Corinthians excelling in?

   What is Paul encouraging them to also excel in?

5. "The gift is acceptable according to _____."

6. II Corinthians 9:7-15 spells out heavenly principles of earthly giving. List these:

Talk to God about your giving. Ask Him if He is pleased. If there is anything that needs to be settled, settle it now!

How the Humble Grateful Heart Gives

1. Ralph Waldo Emerson once said that "Nothing great has ever been achieved without enthusiasm."

    The word *enthusiasm* comes from the ancient Greek *en* and *theos* meaning "in God."

    How can you apply this thought to the practice of "grateful giving?"

2. It has been said that complaining is one of the favorite pastimes of the "self," or the "old man." How can you use the act of grateful giving in a way that strengthens the new creation and cuts off the power of selfishness?

3. Read I Timothy 6:6-10. Re-write this "advice to the not-so-wealthy" in your own words, as if you were giving advice to your own child, or a younger believer.

    How does this advice compare to the attitudes of our culture?

    How does the life of someone who follows this advice look different than the life of someone who is in tune with modern American culture?

4. How does Paul counsel the wealthy to live? (See I Timothy 6:17-19.)

5. Read II Chronicles 31:2-10. Why is it important to give generously, regularly and cheerfully to the work of God?

6. Hosea 9:10 provides a spiritual principle related to consecration. What is it?

In the Beginning, God...

Meditate on the many ways that God is the first and best Giver of gifts.

In the beginning, God...
thoughts from Genesis 1

God is the Creator, the First Cause, the Former-Shaper, the Hovering-Over One;

> *the First Speaker, the Light-Bringer, the Separator of Light from Darkness;*

God is the First Namer, the Judge of what is good;

> *the Imaginer, the Gatherer, the First Gardener.*

God is the Sustainer of Life, the Ritual-Maker,

> *the Marker and Creator of times and days and seasons.*

He is the God of teeming life, the Blesser of life and the living,

> *the Author and Benefactor of fruitfulness and increase,*

> *the Originator of wildness and domesticity, and the Only One who can and has*

> *created the image-bearing process: We are like Him; our children are like us.*

He is the First Delegator, the first Job Fair, the Originator of gender, the First Giver

> *of Gifts.*

God is!

Wisdom: Principles of the Process

II Chronicles Chapter 1 tells the story of Solomon's prayer for wisdom. This is another of those prayers worth adopting as our own. Solomon prayed something like this:

"Lord, you have shown me such great kindness, and you have already given me so much. Give me also wisdom and knowledge to serve you well by serving others well. Without your wisdom I can do absolutely nothing."

What a great prayer! **Knowing that on my own I can do nothing of spiritual significance will help me to cultivate the wisdom of restraint: controlling the impulse to give advice and reproof based on my own immediate reactions and assumptions.**

Solomon had the right idea. He understood that the prayers of his father David, the acceptance of his kingship by all of Israel, his high reputation, were not enough. He was humble enough to know that his greatest need was God's intervention, His supernatural wisdom in ruling Israel well. Praying for wisdom is one of the wisest things we can do, and we need to do it continually in all humility.

The Wisdom of Godly Restraint

When we know we have met God, and we see God at work in our lives, it can be easy to become over-confident of our ability to know the truth about situations and people. Even when God is speaking to us, we can so easily misinterpret and speak out of our own experience, assumptions or judgments. "His ways are far above our ways." We can't assume our thinking is superior to someone else's, or that our opinion is necessarily a reflection of God's will in the situation.

When we respond to others or pray for others in a way that dismisses or minimizes or judges them and their concerns or choices, when we jump in and tell them what to do, it is likely they will feel alone, misunderstood, silenced and judged. If we exhort them to "just pray," or "trust God!" we imply that they are not already doing this, and there is judgment in it. It is unfair to assume that struggles are a result of sin, prayerlessness or a lack of faith. "It is not good to have zeal without knowledge, nor to be hasty and miss the way" (Proverbs 19:2).

Let's be careful here. We are to admonish each other; however, this word, used in Romans 15:14, I Corinthians 10:11, Ephesians 6:4, Colossians 3:16, I Thessalonians 5:12 and II Thessalonians 3:15, means "to call attention to, to *gently* caution or warn."

Even when we see danger in another's choices or attitudes or doctrine, we are to deal with them as members of our family, not as enemies, but as equally capable, not as inferior to us; we speak because we love them and are concerned for them. When there is no sin, just trouble and anxiety, there is no need to reprove, unless God clearly gives the words to say. "Don't be too eager to tell others their faults, for we all make many mistakes" (James 3:1).

Wise restraint does not mean we fail to speak up when we know there is sin in a believer's life. We are accountable, to each other and to God, for speaking warnings and reproof about known sin to each other. Ezekiel 2:16-21 is clear about God's heart on this matter: If, by observation or revelation, we know about sin, yet fall silent and fail to reprove, we are held accountable by God, and judged guilty. We speak the truth in love, and we do not fail to speak it, and speak it clearly. Usually this is done privately.

When we share with each other our hurts and fears and griefs, it is OK to do no more than simply be there for each other and listen. When someone expresses anxiety, rushing in to offer advice or read long Scripture passages is so tempting, but there is no need for us to fill up silence with words. There is no need for us to respond with words at all. There is no need for us to make someone cry or to make them stop crying. We aren't responsible for making them feel better or making them feel worse by telling them what we think they've done wrong to cause all this disaster, or how to fix it. We can trust God to do that, if it needs to be done. *When we are quiet, we give God a chance to truly speak to them or to us. It is an invitation for God to come alongside.*

It has been said that ninety per cent of love is just showing up. That's the most important thing: Just be there and listen. God may want to speak something into their lives through you, but you will never get what it is if you are in a hurry to speak your own words. Give up the idea that you know what they need. *God* knows what they need.

To simply say, "That must be so hard. Can I pray for you?" is a gift of affirmation and comfort that even a non-believer usually won't turn down. A person who is treated in this way feels accepted and heard. This is the way of Love. This is the way of the person on the journey of the fresh-squeezed Life traveled with wisdom.

The wisdom of restraint does not naturally happen to us; it is a supernatural gift to the humble heart that depends on God anew in every situation. One of our biggest enemies is our own over-confidence in our ability to see and convey truth to others, and our own desire to jump in and fix what's wrong. When we speak or pray quickly out of ideas and judgments that come to us immediately, we are in danger of misreading God, running over others and derailing God's work in the situation. It doesn't have to be this way.

Without the humility of acknowledging that human wisdom is insufficient, we usually get it wrong. I think most of us most of the time do not realize to what extent this is true. We give advice to people, we pray for people, and walk away feeling good about ourselves. We never find out that our words were wildly inaccurate, inappropriate, confusing or even demoralizing.

The vast majority of people fall silent when hurt by others, and walk away. When someone is so intent on helping you, it is nearly impossible to say, "Wait a minute. You're wrong about that." In fact, most people would consider it unloving to speak up. They may even consider any "defensiveness" proof that what was said is in fact true.

Since others assume this person is ministering under direction from the Holy Spirit they may further judge you to be rebelling against God. So you keep quiet. When we silence each other like this, we are cutting off our own and each other's growth. If God is in the word spoken, He will provide love and grace in the delivery of it, even if it sharply reproves. **When God breathes out truth to His children who are walking in His ways, however imperfectly, he also breathes out love; that is His essential nature.** Even a warning or a rebuke, when it is delivered by the Holy Spirit, can be received. Even if it hurts, at the same time it heals.

If, as I am listening to someone or praying for someone, a single word intrudes on my thinking, all I have is a word. I want to pad it with a sentence or a paragraph, but all God has given is a word. I must let the word be enough. I may speak the word to the person, and ask its significance. I may speak the word to God in prayer, asking for further guidance. Perhaps all he intends is the single word. I need to let that be enough.

If we feel humble concern or compassion for someone, if we feel afraid for someone's spiritual well-being and believe that God wants us to say something, we need to say it and not be afraid. Boldness to speak the truth is a necessary characteristic of the Spirit-led life. But let's check our own attitude and make sure we are sharing in love, and out of complete dependence on God.

To do the right thing, whether it is to be personally accountable to God for our words, or to speak up when someone thinks they are helping and they are not, or to refrain from speaking so we can listen with all openness when someone else speaks, is wise restraint, but costly. It is truthful. It is honest giving and receiving. It is part of holding each other accountable. It springs from humble gratitude to God for His love for us.

Do we have enough love and wisdom to manage this? Not at all. But God does.

Stop and ask Him right now for the wisdom of restraint. Let God inhabit and live through and speak, through your heart, Life into the lives of others.

The Wisdom of Rest

God has built rest into His plan. The seventh day of the week is a day of rest. The Israelites were instructed to observe a sabbath year of rest for the land every 7th year, not sowing crops during that entire year. After seven "sabbaths" of years, 7x7, or 49 years, they were to observe a year of Jubilee in the 50th year, and announce freedom for slaves, rest from their indentured service (Leviticus 25).

This principle is at work throughout creation in various ways. Bears hibernate over the winter. Many trees and bushes go dormant over the winter, and are pruned back to give the plant rest, which then results in renewed vigor during the warm growing months which follow. We need to respect that God-ordained pattern of activity followed by rest to gain strength for more activity and fruitfulness. God intends for us to respect the need for rest for the worker.

As we enter into relationship with others, we need to give both them and ourselves permission to rest as needed. Not everyone has the same limitations; we are responsible for respecting our own and those of others, no matter how different from ours they may be.

Serving others is rewarding and joyful, if we get the rest along the way that we need. **As much in demand as Jesus was, He honored his own need for rest, and encouraged His disciples to set aside time to rest as well** (see Mark 6:31-32). There are times when God grants a season of rest to seek Him. We need to accept that and not rush on ahead of God and wear ourselves out doing things we are too exhausted to do well. Otherwise, when we need energy and focus for a God-ordained task, we may be spent.

A second type of rest that God has ordained is rest from trouble and attack. When God grants this type of rest, it allows us to accomplish what God wants us to put our hands to.

When, at the close of David's reign as king, Israel experienced the rest of finally being at peace with neighboring kingdoms, the people had the resources, the energy, the focus and the will to think about building the Temple. David knew this and pointed it out to them as he handed over the reins to his son Solomon.

Rest is a God-given blessing; in II Chronicles 14:1-7, we read that Asa king of Judah "did what was good and right in the eyes of the Lord his God," and "No one was at war with him during those years for the Lord gave him rest." Then to make sure we get the connection, verses 7-8 re-state: "'Let us build up these towns,' he said to Judah. 'The land is still ours, because we have sought the Lord our God; **we sought him and he has given us rest on every side**.' So they built and prospered."

The pattern is first obedience to God, then God-given rest from trouble and attack, then building for the kingdom of God!

In addition, it seems wise to pray for rest. If your life consists of constant turmoil or endless toil, and you never have the time to seek or serve God, if you are on the brink of exhaustion and collapse, it's time to pray for rest from endless work and for protection from your enemy. It is not God's will for you to be so overwhelmed by disaster or responsibilities over your whole lifetime that you never have the opportunity to serve God joyfully. Jesus extends this invitation: "Come to me, all you who are weary and burdened, and I will give you rest" (Matthew 11:28). His plan is for you to find your rest in Him.

God, give me the wisdom and blessing of God-ordained rest!

The Wisdom of Godly Repentance

Oh, the wisdom of a tender heart toward God! The moment we realize we have gone off on our own or handled things with someone badly, God wants us to return and repent. "'Even now,' declares the Lord, 'return to me with all your heart,' for He is gracious and compassionate, slow to anger and abounding in love" (Joel 2:12-13).

We sometimes make the mistake of thinking that if we feel the presence of God or if God has been using us, we have nothing to repent of. Wisdom, on the other hand, gives us a sensitive heart toward the nudge, the still, small voice, the feeling of unrest, that is there to get us to stop for a moment and let God show us where we are going wrong. **The closer we get to God, the more even small deviations from His character grieve us and move us to repentance.**

To confess our faults to God and to one another is the way of Love. Our human hearts don't want to admit we are wrong, but the wisdom of godly repentance for our sins and mistakes becomes easier as we practice it. It works in us a maturity of faith that humbly acknowledges our insufficiency and God's all-sufficiency, the supremacy of God's ways and thinking over our own.

We cause God such grief when we neglect repentance for sin; we risk bringing on ourselves tremendous heartache and judgment if we shrug off our awareness of our own sins.

Lord, keep my heart tender toward You, and always quick to confess sin. I want to please you above all else.

The Wisdom of Godly Fear: Reverence

Reverence is the wisdom to submit to God's wisdom, His will, His way, and His worthiness to be worshiped, obeyed, loved and trusted. "The fear of the Lord is the beginning of wisdom" (Proverbs 1:7). This is where it all starts. This wisdom of reverence is the humility to bow before Him as our King, to acknowledge that we don't get to set the standards, make the rules, or have the final say. It is godly wisdom that recognizes His pre-eminence and power.

The wisest decision I ever made was to accept Christ as my Lord and begin the life-journey of re-setting my compass daily to "true North."

Looking back now on many years of walking with God, I see how much wisdom has been worked into my soul because I accepted Christ's Lordship in times of protracted trial and disaster, in times of unbearable grief and repeated wounding. I see also how foolish I still am sometimes, how much I still fall short, fall apart, fall down.

In times of trial, it is the wisdom of humility that accepts God's right to let me suffer, and realizes that it does not take away from His goodness. In times of blessing, it is the wisdom of humility that thanks God, because I know down deep that every good gift is from above. There is no goodness except that which proceeds from God.

Wisdom is not something we can catch like the flu or like enthusiasm at the ballpark; it is not something we earn like an A on a test. It is not something we can put on like a coat, or passively soak up like a sponge does water.

It is something that God works into the fabric of our character as we choose again and again to trust Him, that wild Lion who is also the pure-hearted Lamb.

It is work; we must press in and we must discipline ourselves. **We get more wisdom as we submit to what has already been given.**

Yet it is a gift, a treasure we peel back slowly layer by layer, each layer shining more radiantly with the Light at the center, that sweet, pure, saving, healing Light, Who teaches us wisdom day by day.

There is always a danger that we will become so certain of our own standing with God that we depend on our own thinking, or that we assume others could not be as wise, mature and obedient as we are. A heart full of reverence will help re-orient us to humility of heart and dependence on God.

O God, as I serve You and serve others, give me wisdom! Give me the wisdom of restraint, that I will be willing to wait for Your timing and Your words and Your heart on the matter. Give me the wisdom of rest from the work you give me to do, that I will be careful to care for the body you've given me, so I may continue to serve You. Grant me supernatural rest and protection from the attacks of the enemy. Teach me the wisdom of repentance, a heart that is tender toward You and responsive to Your Spirit, when You show me a word of mine, or a thought or an action, that is not aligned with Your heart. And increase in my heart the wisdom of reverence that worships You as my rightful Lord and King, and bows to Your rule. God, grant me wisdom to serve You and others well. Work in me godly wisdom, so that my relationships and service honor You. Amen.

Godly Restraint

1. Read John 5:30. Explain how Jesus showed us the way of restraining our own thoughts. How did He show restraint?

   He was able to do this by keeping His focus on pleasing _____ and acknowledging that He _____.

2. Proverbs 17:9 warns about a lack of restraint that will ruin relationships. What is it?

3. Proverbs 18:2 names another evidence of lack of restraint. What is it?

   This verse labels someone without restraint as a _____.

4. A lack of restraint usually shows up in the tongue. James 3 describes the tongue. In the first 12 verses, there are 12 descriptions of the tongue. List them here:

5. Starting with verse 13, James explains the remedy for the tongue's potential for evil. He says that true wisdom will be proven in two ways. What are they?

6. Verses 14-18 describe what the foolishness of earthly pride and the wisdom of restraint that comes from God look like. List these characteristics here:

   Worldly "wisdom"   Godly wisdom

Godly Restraint II

1. If we don't restrain our own tongues, what eventually happens?

2. Jeremiah 13:15-17 describes the downfall of those who are proud of their own wisdom and insight, and therefore fail to exercise restraint. Jeremiah warns God's people to _____ and give _____ to God. He says that the result of failing to change their ways will be _____ and _____. Finally they will be _____. Explain in your own words the scriptural principle of the importance of restraint, and the results of ignoring it.

3. What word does I Peter 5:5 use to describe this wisdom of restraint that is the opposite of being proud?

4. Read I Peter 5:8. What word in this verse is another way to describe the wisdom of restraint?

    What is the danger of ignoring it outlined in this verse?

    How does this relate to Jeremiah 13:15-17?

5. How does restraint, or the lack of it, affect the Body of Christ?

6. How are you doing in this area?

Godly Rest

1. Read Genesis 33:12-14. There are three principles of rest that Jacob observed in these verses. Write them down in your own words.

2. Although David often felt overwhelmed and panicked by life's events, he learned how to calm himself down. What does he tell himself in Psalms 116:7?

3. In Isaiah 30:15, God gives instruction to His children, who were trying to protect themselves from their enemies, the Assyrians. They thought they needed to work frantically to achieve peace in their lives, but God points out that their work is of no value unless they also

4. Read Isaiah 32:16-18 and Isaiah 33:15-17. Here God is very clear with His people about how to find rest and peace. Write this principle of rest in your own words.

5. What is the difference between people who find rest and those who don't? (See Jeremiah 6:16.)

6. Where do the people of God find their resting place? (See Jeremiah 50:6-7.)

7. Jesus extends a beautiful invitation to all those who are exhausted and overwhelmed with responsibilities. What does He offer? (Matthew 11:28-30)

   What do we have to do to experience that promise fulfilled in our lives?

8. Read Colossians 3:15. What are we to do with this peace we receive from Christ?

   How does this affect the Body of Christ?

Godly Repentance

1. Some people view repentance as something an unbeliever must do to be forgiven, but as unnecessary for the believer, since Christ died for all our sins, past, present and future. Read Joel 2:12-17. List the types of people God is calling to repentance.

2. Read Revelation 3:1-3. Here God is again calling believers to repentance. What are these believers like?

   What do they need to repent of?

3. Read Revelation 3:14-19. Describe these believers.

   What is God's attitude toward them?

4. Read II Corinthians 7:11. Paul has previously written a letter of rebuke to the Corinthians for tolerating sin in their midst. It was hard for them to hear. Now he points out to them the results of their repentance. What are these results?

5. Jeremiah 31:18-19 is a heartfelt, humble prayer of repentance for sin. What were the consequences of sin?

   Of repentance?

6. In Jeremiah, God declares that Israel has committed two appalling, shocking sins. What are they? (Jeremiah 2:13)

   What is the one thing God wants them to do? (Jeremiah 3:12-13)

7. We typically want to blame a bad childhood or a traumatic experience in life for our sins. Who does God say is responsible? (Jeremiah 4:18)

Godly Repentance II

1. Why do you think believers might need to repent, even though Christ paid the price for all our sins?

2. It is possible for believers to veer so far off course that they participate willingly and knowingly in sin. When that happens, what is God's reaction?

    Hosea 11:7-9: _____

    Hosea 14:1-2: _____

    Jeremiah 6:16-17: _____

    Jeremiah 2:1-3: _____

    Jeremiah 2:35: _____

3. The early church leaders partnered with God in removing sin from within the Body of Christ. How did they do that?

    I Corinthians 5:9-13 _____

    I Corinthians 11:23-32: _____

    II Corinthians 5:20-6:2: _____

    II Corinthians 6:16-7:1: _____

    II Corinthians 7:8-10: _____

    Philippians 4:9: _____

    Acts 5:1-6: _____

4. Repentance is much, much more than just saying we're sorry for our sin. Read Isaiah 58:1-12. Here God spells out just what repentance entails. Write down in your own words how God judges whether or not you are truly sorry.

Godly Fear: Reverence

I Peter 1:15-17 says, "Just as He who called you is holy, so be holy in all you do; for it is written: "Be holy, because I am holy.' Since you call on a Father who judges each man's work impartially, live your lives as strangers here in reverent fear."

Write a prayer below that expresses your reverence and awe of God, and your submission to His will, His way, His wisdom, His worthiness to be worshiped, obeyed, loved and trusted. Spend some time today in His presence, reverencing your Lord and reading aloud your written prayer to Him. Meditate on how He is at work in your life, to conform you to the image of Christ, to refine you like gold in the fire, and to make you a blessing for His glory. Be in awe that the God of the universe wants a relationship with you!

Submission to the Squeezing: The Winepress

Life, pressed down and running over, fresh-squeezed juicy life, comes at a price. The grapes that are full of life, a result of the branch being fully connected to the Vine, are picked, washed, pressed to bursting, squeezed beyond recognition, until all that's left is the essential juice, full of life.

Even when, as a branch, we are fully and continually connected to the Vine, the fruit we produce is a combination of our flesh and God's Spirit. If we allow it, God will use the squeezing we experience in life to refine us, to purge more and more of our flesh, so that more and more it is God's life and sweetness that pour out of us.

Life in the winepress is a place where the flesh gets separated from the Spirit, where the fruit is judged, bruised, purged and refined. This "believers' winepress" is a place of right judgment but not of wrath. This is a place where God shows us our flesh and we humbly repent and submit to His refining work, as He changes us "from glory to glory."

If we surrender to what I am calling the believer's winepress, judging ourselves and confessing our sins to God, we avoid the winepress of His judgment here on earth as His children. "If we judged ourselves, we would not come under judgment" (I Corinthians 11:31).

When we don't judge ourselves, we risk bringing judgment on ourselves; this is called the Lord's Winepress in Lamentations. Even then, however, "when we are judged by the Lord, we are being disciplined so that we will not be condemned with the world" (I Corinthians 11:32). This righteous judgment of God against us when we sin creates tremendous suffering, weeping, broken relationships, captivity, mourning, bitterness, weakness, misery, and pollution (see Lamentations 1-2). "In His winepress the Lord has trampled the Virgin Daughter of Judah" (1:15).

We may experience this winepress even if we are not the ones in rebellion. Jeremiah the prophet suffered terribly as he watched the punishment of Israel: "This is why I weep and my eyes overflow with tears. No one is near to comfort me, no one to restore my spirit. My children are destitute because the enemy has prevailed" (verse 16).

The purpose of the Lord's Winepress is to bring the straying one to repentance and back into right relationship with God.

Going to church, naming the Name, is not enough. Rehoboam, Solomon's son who became king after him, "did evil, for he *did not set his heart* to seek the Lord" (II Chronicles 12:14). *That's all it takes for us to do evil.* We don't have to intend it or plan it. To do evil in God's sight starts with merely neglecting to set our hearts to seek God. In order to avoid doing evil, we must *set our hearts* to seek God. This is not a relaxed receiving. This is a passionate and purposeful pursuing.

The grapes of earth are destined for wrath (Revelation 14:14-19; 19:15); this is the final Winepress of God's Wrath. But the purpose of the believers winepress or the Lord's Winepress on earth is always increased fruitfulness: "He cuts off every branch in me that bears no fruit, while every branch that does bear fruit he prunes so that it will be even more fruitful" (John 15:2). So we submit to this winepress, for this pleases the Vinedresser, and we know an increased harvest will result.

Experiencing the winepress here on earth, then, can take several forms: unavoidable suffering; or judging ourselves by the Word of God; or the pain of experiencing God's correction. What does it mean to submit to this winepress? **First, submission means that our attitude is one of humble acceptance rather than pride, denial, or resentment.** David says that the rebuke of a righteous man is actually a kindness, and not to be refused (Psalms 141:5). James goes so far as to say that we should be downright joyful when we face various trials (1:5). So whether the correction comes from godly believers, or from God Himself, or from trials that are part of the trouble Christ told us we would surely experience on earth, we can trust that God loves us and will take care of us, and that He will go even further, and actually use our suffering for our good and His glory.

In his walk with God, David also learns that **when the sorrows and disasters of life overwhelm us to the point where we can't take another step, we can still remind ourselves of God's goodness; we can choose to think about what God has done in the past; and we can still pray.** We tend to get angry, or to curl up, go numb, and pull away from God. Listen to David's reaction: "The enemy pursues me, he crushes me to the ground; he makes me dwell in darkness like those long dead. So my spirit grows faint within me; my heart within me is dismayed. I remember the days of long ago; I meditate on all your works and consider what your hands have done. I spread out my hands to you; my soul thirsts for you like a parched land. I have put my trust in you. Show me the way I should go. Rescue me from my enemies, O Lord, for I hide myself in you" (from Psalms 143:4-9). He *pursues* God. First, he pours out his complaints and his agony to a God who cares; then he makes a choice to think instead of God's character and His track record of taking care of His people. He asks for guidance, and expresses his faith, even when he doesn't see how God will deliver him. We, too, have a choice about how we will deal with life's most difficult seasons. **When life is unbearable, we can run to a God who is trustworthy.**

Our times of squeezing are intended to work in us compassion instead of judgment toward others. "Praise be to the God and Father of our Lord Jesus Christ, the Father of compassion and the God of all comfort, who comforts us in all our troubles, *so that we can comfort those in any trouble* with the comfort we ourselves have received from God. For just as the sufferings of Christ flow over into our lives, so also through Christ our comfort overflows" (II Corinthians

1:3-5). We know what it feels like to suffer, so our hearts open wider to the plight of others in their suffering, and we yearn for their restoration to blessing and fruitful ministry. We see their blind spots, and the specks in their eyes, and we feel compassion, because we are painfully aware of the logs that have been in our own eyes, and we know there are still areas of our lives that are "under construction."

While we are honest with God about our feelings, we don't lapse into self-pity. Being a victim has become very popular in our culture. It is common to blame a bad childhood or bad genes for our bad choices. Criticizing, judging and blaming others, pouting or "priding," is the easy way out, and it stunts our growth. Submitting to life's squeezing means that we take responsibility for our own choices while maintaining a humble grateful heart toward God. It means that even if we are suffering through no fault of our own, we maintain our trust in God, whose heart it is to restore and redeem.

While we may feel intense grief in our suffering, this does not define who we are. It may be where we are at this moment, and it is important to allow ourselves to go through the grieving process, which takes time. But we are cooperating with God to move beyond that, to a place of joy and productivity in the kingdom of God. Wallowing in our pain will drive others away eventually, even though for a season it can get a lot of attention and sympathy. Self-pity does not proceed from faith, and it does not work the works of God. At some point, preferably sooner rather than later, **we come to a place of looking forward instead of back, a place of faith, joy, peace, love, gratitude and service.**

David, when he finds himself surrounded by liars and deceivers, when he sees that he is living in a world in which "the wicked freely strut about," testifies to the preciousness of God's Word in the midst of his intense suffering. "The words of the Lord are flawless, like silver refined in a furnace of clay purified seven times" (Psalms 12:6). This verse is plunked down in the middle of a short psalm that is otherwise a lament about the presence of evil in the world, and its terrible effect on innocent people.

Where is the silver refined? In a furnace of clay. "We have this treasure in jars of clay to show that this all-surpassing power is from God and not from us. We are hard-pressed on every side, but not crushed; perplexed, but not in despair; persecuted, but not abandoned; struck down, but not destroyed. We always carry around in our body the death of Jesus, so that the life of Jesus may also be revealed in our body" (II Corinthians 4:7-10).

When life becomes a furnace, when things are so overwhelming that we feel as if we are not only *in* the furnace but have ourselves *become* the unbearably hot furnace, let's put God's Word, already pure and perfect, into the furnace. There, our understanding of God and His Word will be purified and perfected. We ourselves, as our imperfections and misunderstandings about God are burned away, show more and more His beauty, and know more and more the weakness and insufficiency of our own flesh. As we see our own weakness, we have more compassion on others in their weakness. **This is how the terrible things we go through in life are redeemed: we let God's Word in us do its work. In order for the Word to "dwell in you richly," you must "hide His Word in your heart" (Psalms 119:11).** *Put the silver into the furnace.*

The Purpose of the Winepress: Refining and Purging

1. Read Isaiah 48:8-18 (and Deuteronomy 8:3, 5). Here God explains the purpose of "the furnace of affliction." When we go through hard times, we are being _____. Look up the word in the dictionary and write the definition here.

2. In verse 10, God says He couldn't refine His people and get _____, as He intended. What is the reason He could find nothing valuable left after they had been tested? (See verses 8, 18)

3. Read James 4:7-10. List what James tells us to do in trials and temptations.

    Now list what will happen if we do these things.

4. I Peter 1:6-9 tells us, "You may have had to suffer grief in all kinds of trials. These have come so that your faith, of greater worth than gold, which perishes even though refined by fire, may be proved genuine and may result in praise, glory and honor when Jesus Christ is revealed." How can you allow the difficulties of life to do this work in you?

5. The purpose of the refiner's fire is always to burn out impurities and reveal the precious metal within. I Peter 1:22 says we purify ourselves by _____ . When we do this, we will have genuine brotherly love [phileo.] Peter doesn't stop there, but urges us to [agape], or _____. If we, as members of the Body of Christ, live by this verse, *what will it look like?*

The Believer's Winepress

1. In the winepress, the grapes are bruised and crushed to extract the precious juice. Read Isaiah 53:1-6. Who experienced the winepress of life before you did?

2. Read Isaiah 42:1-3. This passage reveals Christ's treatment of bruised ones: those who have been in life's crushing winepress. How would you describe it?

3. In Luke 4:18, we find Jesus teaching in the temple, reading scripture to reveal that he is the one who "sets at liberty them that are bruised." If you have been bound and bruised in the hard times of your life, stop right now and thank Jesus that He is the one who brings deliverance and healing; ask Him to complete His work of liberty in you. *Ask Him!*

4. The bruising and crushing of the winepress is only one picture in scripture that describes our experience of hardship here on earth. Read John 15:1-8. How does Jesus describe the relationships among the Father, Jesus and us?

   What happens to every branch?

   When a living, fruitful branch is cut, what is the purpose?

   What would you say is the role of the branch; what does it do?

5. What is often the cutting instrument of the Gardener, or, in Hebrews 4:12, what is the sword?

   List all the words in Hebrews 4:12-13 that describe this sword.

   Now list what it does.

6. It's hard to imagine that the Son of God would submit himself to the winepress, or that His Father would ask that of Him, but that is how much we are loved. Jesus submitted to the crushing He was appointed to. Read Hebrews 5:7-10. How did he handle what he went through?

   What was the result?

Increased Fruitfulness

1. Read Matthew 3:1-10. John the Baptist challenges the religious elite to "produce fruit in keeping with repentance." What kind of fruit is he talking about?

    Verse 10 warns that any "tree that does not produce good fruit will be cut down and thrown into the fire." What do you think he means?

2. In Matthew 12:33-34, Jesus says that "a tree is recognized by its fruit. For out of the overflow of the heart the mouth speaks. The good man brings good things out of the good stored up in him." From this passage, write down your definition of "fruit."

3. Read Mark 4:1-20. In order to bear fruit, we must be on guard against _____; we must be sure to grow deep _____; we must not be distracted from our relationship with God by _____, _____, or _____.

4. In John 15:16, Jesus tells his disciples, "I chose you and appointed you to go and bear fruit, fruit that will last." How important then is it to bear fruit?

    What is "fruit that will last?"

5. In Romans 6:22, fruit is described as resulting in holiness and eternal life; in Romans 15:28, fruit refers to the giving of material blessings by the church to the poor; in Philippians 1:22, fruit is the result of work done for Christ; in Hebrews 13:15, fruit is sacrificial praise and thankfulness toward God; in James 3:18, the fruit harvested is righteousness that results from being a peacemaker. What do all these different types of fruit have in common?

6. How do we produce this fruit that will last?

    First, we choose to _____ (Galatians 5:16).

    Then we submit to _____ by _____ (John 15:2), so that we will be even more fruitful.

7. 7. "A tree is known by its fruit." This is how we know we are living in the Spirit: We bear the fruit of the Spirit. List these manifestations of fruit (Galatians 5:22-25):

8. 8. Are you willing to go under the Gardener's knife to become more fruitful for Him? List the ways you can cooperate with the Master Gardener's pruning in your life:

Increased Compassion

1. Read Psalms 86:15. What is the result of God's compassion toward us?

2. Read Lamentations 3:32-33. If you are in a season of grief and hardship, how do these verses bring comfort and reassurance? What is in God's heart toward you?

3. We are made in the image of God; therefore, just as God is capable of compassion, so are we. Read Isaiah 49:15-16. To help us understand the depths of God's compassion toward us, how is it described in this passage?

4. Think of a time that you were able to have compassion on someone else because you had been through something similar. Describe how that happened.

5. Do you think it is necessary to have the exact experiences as others in order to feel compassion for them? Explain your thinking.

6. Two people who go through the same difficulty may not react the same; one may express greater compassion toward others as a result, while the other may not. What do you think makes the difference?

7. Read these verses, and list the reasons Jesus had compassion.

   Matthew 9:35-36 _____

   Matthew 14:14 _____

   Matthew 15:32 _____

   Matthew 20:29-34 _____

   Mark 9:14-27 _____

   Luke 7:11-15 _____

Spend some time in prayer, asking God to show you if you have compassion for people like those above. Ask yourself if any of these problems make you uncomfortable or judgmental. Ask God to give you His heart of compassion toward others.

Pressing Forward: Keep Moving, Growing, Becoming, Accepting, Submitting, Praising

The apostle Paul expresses the attitude of one who has been through tremendous hardship and loss, yet becomes stronger and more godly instead of staying overwhelmed:

"Whatever was to my profit I now consider loss for the sake of Christ. What is more, I consider everything a loss compared to the surpassing greatness of knowing Christ Jesus my Lord, for whose sake I have lost all things. I consider them rubbish, that I may gain Christ and be found in him, not having a righteousness of my own that comes from the law, but that which is through faith in Christ, the righteousness that comes from God and is by faith. I want to know Christ and the power of his resurrection and the fellowship of sharing in his sufferings, becoming like him in his death, and so, somehow, to attain to the resurrection from the dead. Not that I have already obtained all this, or have already been made perfect, but I press on to take hold of that for which Christ Jesus took hold of me. I do not consider myself yet to have taken hold of it. But one thing I do: Forgetting what is behind and straining toward what is ahead, I press on toward the goal to win the prize for which God has called me heavenward in Christ Jesus" (Philippians 3:7-14).

Make this passage your own. Read into it your own losses and griefs and sufferings. Pray it, meditate on it, claim it, read it, day after day, as you reach toward greater godliness, compassion, and fruitfulness in Him. Praise Him for what He is working in you. Use the rest of this page to journal your experience with this passage.

Participating in the Divine Nature

Read II Peter 1:3-8. Peter made a mess of things many times. If he can come to the place of maturity he describes in these verses, so can we. These verses tell us that we can actually participate in the divine nature of God! They tell us how this comes about, and what we can do to cooperate with God in this. Which of the qualities mentioned in these verses are you lacking?

Ask God to help you in these areas.

Which of these qualities do you have?

Peter tells us to not be satisfied with where we are now, but to "possess these qualities in increasing measure." What will be the result if we do this?

How do you think developing these qualities will affect our relationships within the Body of Christ? Spend some time imagining how our relationships will be different if we are developing the virtues mentioned. Write down your thoughts here about each quality Peter lists.

Building on the Dust of the Past: The Temple

We have followed the story of David and his longing to build the Temple, and how he lovingly laid up treasure upon treasure in storehouses, preparing for the day the Temple would actually be built. We have seen that Solomon his son took his responsibilities as king so seriously that, when God told him he could have anything we wanted, Solomon asked for wisdom to be a better king.

"Then Solomon began to build the temple of the Lord in Jerusalem on Mount Moriah. It was on the threshing floor of Araunah" (II Chronicles 3:1).

Remember that the threshing floor of Araunah was a place of desperation and grief, where David offered sacrifices to God in repentance for his sin, and begged God to turn away his punishment, which was affecting all of Israel (I Chronicles 21).

Look at how this story has come full circle! Solomon with all his power and wealth, and any location at his disposal as king, chooses to build the Temple in a place of humility, tears and repentance, a place where God met the destitute, grief-stricken sinner with grace and mercy. In God's economy, the place of worship is always built on the tears of repentance and humility before a holy God.

Because David his father had lived out the end of his life with godly love, Solomon had heard this story. David had not held it back for fear it would make him look bad. The perfect love of his Father had cast out fear (I John 4:18). It is *costly* to tell the truth about ourselves and our past. We may get rejected or judged by others. Our pride takes a beating. It is hard to be this open, this vulnerable. But it is a necessary ingredient of the fresh-squeezed life.

David was *accountable*. He told the truth about himself. Here we find Solomon taking that truth to heart. It was a way of humbly honoring this story from the past and acknowledging that no one, not even a king whom God loves, can afford to be confident of his own ability to figure things out, to handle things, to be good enough, on his own.

David gave costly worship and sacrifice to God, and opened up his heart to receive forgiveness from God. Out of a *grateful, humble heart*, he determined that one day, a temple would be built on the dust of the threshing floor of Araunah.

The great magnificent Temple of the Living God was built on a threshing floor, a place of separation and judgment. It was built on a makeshift altar, a place of sacrifice and desperation and tears. It was built on a place arrived at after much suffering and death.

So when we find ourselves on the threshing floor, what do we do? We let the Thresher do His work in us. We let Him glean what is good, and let the rest fall; it is the chaff that blows away, then settles as dust under our feet. What is dust good for? What do you do with it? Build on it. If you don't, a drought of the soul and the winds of adversity may turn the dust of the past into a Dust Bowl. So instead, build.

Solomon built the Temple, a holy place of worship, on the dust of Israel's past. It was built on a place of repentance and mercy, a place of forgiveness and of answered prayer. It was built on a place of restoration of right relationship between God and man. What a beautiful, humble, reverent act it was for Solomon to choose this site. Finally, David's vision of this place of both grief and gleaning being redeemed for God's glory was becoming reality! It must have brought God's heart much pleasure to see this place of agony and tears transformed into a place of worship and joy.

The Temple was a precious and holy place; Solomon took care to express reverence for the Most High God in every detail of the building of the Temple. "He overlaid the inside with pure gold. He built the Most Holy Place. He overlaid the inside with gold" (II Chronicles 3:4,8).

In the new covenant, your body is now the Temple of the Living God (I Corinthians 3:16). Have you come through much suffering? Through many tears? Has your heart cried out for forgiveness? Have you without reserve opened your heart to God, and in openness received His grace and love?

Then you are standing in the place of gleaning, the place of sacrifice, the place where you will meet with God; this is both threshing floor and Holy of Holies. The grain will here be separated from the chaff in your heart and life. Let the chaff go. Let it go.

Let God do His work. It will cost you. You will feel the pain of it. But it is here where God meets you that your King is preparing to overlay your innermost being with pure gold. He is building a Most Holy Place.

Be still, and listen. Your King is here.

O Lord, remember me and the hardships I endured. I make a vow to you: as I enter my house or go to my bed, I find in my heart a dwelling place for You. Arise, Lord, come to your dwelling place. May it be a place of beauty and holiness where you can rest. May I be clothed with your righteousness, and may I sing for joy. For my sake, do not reject me or take away the anointing of Your Spirit, for You have chosen me; You have desired me for Your dwelling place. Here You will sit enthroned because that is what You most want. You bless me with abundance, both spiritually and physically. You clothe my enemies with shame, but you crown me with your loveliness (Psalms 132, paraphrased).

Gleaning the Good Means Sifting Out the Chaff

1. God's refining, purifying work in his people's lives is compared throughout scripture to **threshing** grain, **pruning** fruit-bearing vines, **the winepress**, and testing precious metals in **the furnace**. It always involves getting rid of impurity and that which is worthless, so that what remains is valuable and useful. Which of these metaphors speaks to you?

   What about this metaphor makes sense to you?

   What emotional reactions do you have when you meditate on God's purifying work in your life?

2. The Temple was built on the threshing floor. How does this idea relate specifically to you, with your particular life experience, in your spiritual walk? Be specific.

3. The Temple was built on an altar of desperate prayer and sacrifice. How does this relate to your experience?

4. The Temple was built on an altar of tears and repentance. How does your experience relate to this?

Submitting to the Refiner

The metaphors of gleaning, pruning, pressing and refining express the intention of the work God does in our lives, but there is a difference: The wheat, the grapevines, the grapes and the gold, have no power to resist. We do. God has given us the power to refuse to allow His Word and our life experiences to produce His desired effect.

Describe a time in your life when you did not submit to what God was trying to do in you.

Describe an experience you have had with submitting to God's refining work.

What did God work in you through this time of testing?

Proverbs 17:3 comments, "A hot furnace tests silver and gold, but the Lord tests hearts." Malachi 3:2 asks the question, "Who can endure the day of his coming? Who can stand when he appears? For he will be like a refiner's fire." *Oh, let us submit to His refining work now!*

The Dust

1. Look back on your life, and list the events that have caused destruction, the times you felt that all that was left was ashes.

2. Has God built something on that dust of your past?

   Write down what He has restored or transformed or built in the wake of disaster.

3. Meditate for a moment on how you have been changed, areas in which you have gained compassion or wisdom, because of what you have experienced. How might God use you for His glory in a greater way because of what you've been through?

4. Perhaps you feel too weak and worn out to be of value in God's kingdom. In Psalms 102, David cries out, "I am in distress. For my days vanish like smoke. My heart is blighted and withered like grass." If you feel like David did, ask God to somehow use this time in your life to bring Him glory, and to conform you to His image. He will delight to build something beautiful: "[The Lord] has compassion on those who fear him; for he knows how we are formed, he remembers that we are dust" (Psalms 103:14).

So even if you feel like nothing but dust, pray, *Here I am, Lord; build here."*

Beauty for Ashes

1. Isaiah 61 proclaims the mission Jesus came to earth for. The first three verses tell us that God anointed Him to "preach good news to the poor, to bind up the brokenhearted, to proclaim freedom for the captives and release from darkness for the prisoners, to proclaim the year of the Lord's favor and the day of vengeance of our God, to comfort all who mourn and provide for those who grieve in Zion: to bestow on them a crown of beauty instead of ashes, the oil of gladness instead of mourning, and a garment of praise instead of a spirit of despair."

From the above list, what has God already done for you?

What are you now asking for?

The work of God on earth continues through His Body. Read this list from Isaiah 61 again. In which of these ways is God already using you to glorify Him and bless others? Give examples and be specific.

In which of these ways do you long to be used by God?

Spend some time in worship and prayer, offering yourself for His service and asking God to bring opportunities.

The rest of the chapter goes on to use more words that describe what God wants to do for His people: **rebuild, restore, renew, inheritance, double portion, riches, joy, blessed, salvation, righteousness.**

Use these words in your own prayer of thanksgiving and prayer. Write it down here, then pray it out loud. Confess these powerful words out loud daily; allow God to speak life into your heart!

The Holy Place

Stop several times during the day today to pray this prayer of reverent submission to, and humble gratitude for, God's refining work in your life. Rest in His gentle presence. As you gaze into His eyes, and bow to His work in your life, you are becoming more and more like Him!

Holy, Holy, Holy

My Father in Heaven, even your name breathed out is holy,
a consuming fire that searches out dross.
You are the forest fire, and when you are through,
everything is ash and soot, silence and smoke.
I've heard that wise farmers, if necessary,
burn their land to birth a forest.
My Father in Heaven, even your name is set apart,
distinct from every other name.
You are holy sweetness pouring down,
rinsing me free of all that clings to me,
of all I cling to.
You are the swollen creek that sweeps me off the bank,
the bank itself crumbling,
as I clutch in terror for solid ground.
You are my watery tomb from which I emerge new,
re-patterned again and again.
My Father in Heaven, your name on my lips is a holy song,
a song of entreaty and praise.
The song in my heart toward you grows long;
I need so much from you.
When I stop singing and listen,
my name on your lips is a song of entreaty,
a song of the lover searching for the beloved.
It is a song that I hear through many little deaths,
through flame and flood.
It is the song my heart loves,
and it is enough.

The Temple

I Corinthians 6:19-20 says, "You should know that your body is a temple for the Holy Spirit who is in you. You have received the Holy Spirit from God, so you do not belong to yourselves, because you were bought by God for a price. So honor God with your bodies." Write your thoughts about this.

In Isaiah 60:7, God says to Israel of the literal temple, "I will make my beautiful temple more beautiful." In I Corinthians 3:16-17, Paul writes, "Don't you know that you are God's temple and that God's Spirit lives in you? If anyone destroys God's temple, God will destroy that person, because God's temple is holy and you are that temple." Considering both of these passages, write down your understanding of God's heart toward His temple.

What do you think it means for us today that the Holy of Holies in the original temple was overlaid on the inside with pure gold?

The Word of God speaks of the literal, physical temple, and it speaks of the "temple" of the believer, that is, the physical body. There is another use of the concept of the temple. Look up Ephesians 2:19-21. What is the temple described in this passage?

What does this mean for the church today?

Hebrews 9 lays out for us another use of the word "temple," and what it means for us. Read this passage. What is the temple in these verses?

Who entered it?
What did He bring?
How are we made righteous (overlaid with gold) by faith?
How does this relate to the other uses of the word *temple*?

Discernment in Battle: I Have Seen the Enemy, and He is not You!

"Finally, be strong in the Lord and in his mighty power. Put on the full armor of God so that you can take your stand against the devil's schemes. For our struggle is not against flesh and blood, but against the rulers, against the authorities, against the powers of this dark world and against the spiritual forces of evil in the heavenly realms. Therefore put on the full armor of God, so that when the day of evil comes, you may be able to stand your ground, and after you have done everything, to stand.

"Stand firm then, with the belt of truth buckled around your waist, with the breastplate of righteousness in place, and with your feet fitted with the readiness that comes from the gospel of peace. In addition to all of this, take up the shield of faith, with which you can extinguish all the flaming arrows of the evil one. Take the helmet of salvation and the sword of the Spirit, which is the word of God. And pray in the Spirit on all occasions with all kinds of prayers and requests. With this in mind, be alert and always keep on praying for all the saints" (Ephesians 6:10-18).

Life feels like a war sometimes. We wonder why. We're being nice and fair and good-hearted, and still so much goes wrong! We shouldn't be surprised or confused. There is a real enemy, and there is a real war going on. Our struggle is a daily one, but "our struggle is *not* against flesh and blood." Being earth-bound, we tend to believe what we see and hear and feel. What we experience is that certain people seem to be at war with us! This is not the most important part of the story. The most important part is what is going on beneath and behind, the part that is in the spirit world, which can only be spiritually discerned and spiritually conquered.

So the first rule of this warfare is that we are not at war with flesh and blood. Not really. It may look like that, and it may sound like that, and it may feel like that. This is a fact we need to remind ourselves of, for we most naturally see a person who is working against us in some way as the source of our problem. The person who is fighting you believes there is a valid reason for fighting. What is really at the root of it though is spiritual unrest and mutiny against God *in the spirit world,* and an intention *by Satan* to render you useless to God's kingdom. This is all happening in the world we do not see, and the person cooperating with this plan to derail you has no idea, and

111

maybe you have had no idea either, that this is what happening. In fact, it could be that neither of you is in the wrong, but Satan has found a way to stir up trouble and cause division.

We know the end of the story; God has already triumphed over Satan. In fact, it was never a nail-biter. Satan is a created being, formed by God for good, who chose to rebel. He has an inflated view of himself, and thinks he is a worthy opponent to the God of the universe, so he keeps fighting. It is possible for Satan to win skirmishes, and he does it all the time, because we human beings in our fallen state gravitate toward pride and sin and selfishness, which is Satan's arena. What can we do to be sure we cooperate with God and not Satan? *Put on the whole armor of God.*

The first thing to do is to **stand firm**. When I read these words, I picture a strong, muscled soldier standing in full battle gear, determination in his eyes, with his feet firmly planted, knees slightly bent, ready for action. We are to be prepared for a battle, alert, watching for our "adversary the devil [who] prowls around like a roaring lion, seeking someone to devour" (I Peter 5:8). We are to expect resistance, if we are on God's side and making steps toward faith and obedience and service in His kingdom.

The "belt of truth" must be in place, for this holds everything else in correct position for maximum protection. We must **know the truth**, believe it, and act on it, for it is the truth that sets us free and makes us clean. (See John 8:32, 15:3 and 17:7.) The truth is in the Word of God; the more time we spend in the Word of God, the more securely this belt is fastened.

Knowing the Word does no good though if we don't **take it to heart**. The heart is what is protected by the breastplate. Our hearts are protected from fatal injury by the "breastplate of righteousness." There are two aspects to this righteousness. The first is that we have righteousness, or "right standing" with God, only through the covering of the blood of Jesus shed for our sins. We must have accepted his sacrifice for us. Yet we must also have accepted his Lordship in our lives, and this is the second layer of the breastplate, the true test that reveals whether or not our faith in Christ is real: "If you love me, you will keep my commandments," Jesus tells us (John 14:15). *If we are not walking in the light we have, our ability to ward off the enemy's blows will be compromised, and our hearts are in jeopardy.* Applying His Word to our own lives, acting on it daily, is absolutely essential.

Next we check to be sure we have our feet protected and ready for rough terrain, covered with "the gospel of peace." What an ironic thing it is, that we get ready for war by putting on the gospel of peace. Here's why: While we will need to fight Satan in order to complete our mission, our mission is not to fight, but to **bring the gospel of peace to everyone**, "for He is our peace, who has made us both one, and has broken down the dividing wall of hostility...so making peace, and [reconciling] us both to God in one body through the cross, thereby bringing the hostility to an end" (Ephesians 2:14, 15b-16). *We should not be at war with each other,* angry, refusing to forgive, gossiping, or resenting each other because we don't have something someone else has. Christ came to end hostility: between God and man, and between you and me. We can be at peace with each other and with God through the blood of Jesus Christ. We must let Him be our Prince of Peace!

During war, your body will not take any direct hits if you can use your shield expertly. Your shield of faith in spiritual warfare is made strong only through a personal relationship with Christ. This shield is unusual by earthly standards, because as you use it and test it and see its effectiveness, it grows stronger. This is one reason you can "count it all joy" (James 1:2) when your faith is tested by difficult circumstances and difficult people, because as you **use this shield of faith**, your faith grows and becomes better able to protect you from the shots Satan takes at you.

Your mind is protected by your helmet. Unless we live out daily a salvation relationship with Jesus Christ, our minds will be vulnerable to errors in thinking and doctrine. We will be easy prey for depression, bitterness, anxiety, getting stuck in a victim mentality, perversity, addiction or any other weapons in Satan's arsenal intended to affect our thinking. Instead, "**set your minds on things that are above**, not on things that are on earth. For you have died, and your life is hid with Christ in God. Put to death therefore what is earthly in you: immorality, impurity, passion, evil desire, and covetousness, which is idolatry...anger, wrath, malice, slander, and foul talk. Do not lie to one another, seeing that you have put off the old nature with its practices and have put on the new nature, which is being renewed in knowledge after the image of its creator" (Colossians 3:2-3, 5, 8-10). "Therefore we must pay the closer attention to what we have heard, lest we drift away from it. How shall we escape if we neglect such a great salvation?" (Hebrews 2:1, 3).

I sometimes hear Christians say that their relationship with God is more important than spiritual disciplines like daily Bible reading. This is a faulty and unnecessary either/or choice. It's not either/or, but both/and. Reading the Word is a huge part of developing a relationship with God, not some tedious, separate requirement. How do we test our own thoughts and intentions? How do we test the advice of others? How do we know how to encourage and edify others? By immersing ourselves in the Word. How do we learn God's heart and discern His character? How do we most often hear his voice? How do we become more and more like Him? By opening our hearts to His Word. This is the operator's manual, the battle plan, the treasure map. *This is how we protect our mind: Fill it with God's Word.* Working out our own salvation with fear and trembling, continually and intentionally, we keep our mind protected from Satan's attempts to disable our minds and disorder our thinking.

Now that we are fully protected in our defense against aggression from our enemy, we are to go on the attack against our enemy, and bring the kingdom of light into the kingdom of the surrounding darkness. Our primary offensive weapon is our sword, the Word of God. The only way we can wield this sword well is to have it constantly at our disposal, and to practice using it. As we read and hear and study and memorize the Word of God, as we meditate on it and apply it to our lives, it becomes a part of us. God will bring it to our minds when we need it, so that we are ready for any challenges to our faith. The Word of God is powerful, "sharper than any two-edged sword, piercing to the division of soul and spirit, of joints and marrow, and discerning the thoughts and intentions of the heart. And before him no creature is hidden, but all are open and laid bare to the eyes of him with whom we have to do" (Hebrews 4:12-13). The Word of God is the truth and it reveals the truth, to us and to others. We **resist the lies of Satan by speaking the truth of the Word** into the lives of others. We resist the lies of Satan by speaking the truth of the Word into

our own lives. We resist the attacks of Satan by speaking the truth of the Word out loud directly to him. When we resist him, he *must* flee from us. Light is stronger than darkness.

We are to **pray in the Spirit all the time**; this is both defense and offense against our enemy. Our concern is not to be for ourselves alone, but also for others. Staying aware of all these things, we also **pray for our brothers and sisters in Christ**. This is part of what it means to function in community in the body of Christ. This is part of God's will for our lives. This is a part of living out our mission on this earth as Christians.

"Whatever happens, **conduct yourselves in a manner worthy of the gospel of Christ**" (Philippians 1:27). Our goal is to act in accord with the faith, peace, love and joy of our salvation. This does not mean that we never take decisive action, or speak words that are hard to hear. In fact, in many situations it will mean just the opposite. Jesus overturned the tables of the money-changers in the temple. The apostles told the chief priests, "We must obey God rather than men," then reminded them that they had killed Jesus (Acts 5:29-33). This predictably enraged the chief priests to the point of murderous intent. **The truth is the truth, even when it's not well-received, and we are to speak the truth of God's Word with all boldness**. The apostles were beaten for their boldness in speaking the truth, yet they went away rejoicing (verses 40-41), because it was such an honor to suffer for the advancement of the Kingdom of Christ. Yet there is a caution here: We are to speak the truth *from the heart* (Psalms 15:2), not just from the mind. Speaking the truth without love, from an attitude of argumentativeness or superiority, will not bear the Kingdom's fruit. Oh, let us be led by the Spirit, and motivated and stirred by godly love and longing for all to be brought into the fold, and by a determined yet sweet yearning for God's truth to triumph.

Have you met your enemy? Have you felt the oppression of his attacks against you? I know I have met the enemy, and I know that he is not you! You are my fellow soldier, fighting the same war against the same enemy. We are on the same side. There have been times I have forgotten this. I need to remind myself daily, making sure my armor is in place, that I have only one enemy, and he is most definitely not you.

My enemy is not the person who does not yet believe in God; he is not the one who has a different political stance than I do. He is not even the one who ridicules my faith or intentionally acts to hurt me in some way. My only true enemy exists in the realm of spiritual darkness, and is himself spirit. The only way to fight him is to address him in the spiritual realm, by putting on my armor and praying constantly.

When we have conflict with each other, the Word is very clear about what we are to do. If we keep in mind that you and I are not enemies, we will be able to obey the Word "in a manner worthy of the gospel," and move toward unity and peace within the Body, and so bring honor and praise to God.

Discernment

1. In Solomon's prayer for wisdom, he asks for a "*discerning* heart...to distinguish between right and wrong" (I Kings 3:9). Discernment goes beyond just "knowing;" it involves considering, feeling, thinking about things, and having understanding. He asks for a discerning *heart*; he desires to go beyond his intelligence. The word used for "heart," indicates feelings, the will, the intellect, the *center*. It is as if Solomon is saying, "Let this ability to discern evil when I see it, to discern good when I see it, let this discernment be at the center of my being, so that it determines my attitudes, feelings, actions and judgments." Meditate for a few moments on what it would be like for that to be true of you in life's most trying moments.

2. Read Hebrews 5:11-14. What is our responsibility in obtaining discernment?

3. I Corinthians 12:1-11 speaks about spiritual gifts; one of them is "discernment of spirits." What is the difference between these two types of discernment?

4. Read the following scriptures. List the specific reasons it is important for us to recognize the works of the enemy.

   I Corinthians 7:5

   II Corinthians 2:11

   II Corinthians 11:14

   II Corinthians 12:7

   I Thessalonians 2:18

   II Thessalonians 2:9

   I Peter 5:8

   Matthew 12:22

   Luke 8:12

   Ephesians 4:27

   I Timothy 3:6-7

The Role of the Word

1. What do you think it means to "stand firm?" (See also II Ti 2:15 and 4:5.)

1. Explain the steps you think you need to follow to "put on the belt of truth."

1. Psalms 119 is a lengthy description of David's experience with the Word of God. What is to be the believer's response to the Word (verses 1-4)?

   What is David's lament with regard to the Word (verse 5)?

   Knowing these things about himself and the Word, what does David resolve to do (see verses 7-16)?

   Take a moment to evaluate your experience with God's Word on the basis of these verses. What is true of you?

   What is not yet true of you?

   Is the Word your "counselor" (see verse 24)? Explain your understanding of this.

   Describe what the Word does for David, and decide whether the Word does this for you.

verse	what God's Word does	Does it do this for me?
28		
45		
49		
50		
53		
54		

War and Peace

1. The church has sometimes been guilty of waging war, speaking venomous words, and completely rejecting certain segments of society. List some examples of this:

2. How do you think God feels about this?

3. Is is possible to "love the sinner and hate the sin?" If so, how does this look? Be specific.

4. The scriptures pointedly and repeatedly say that this gospel is for *everyone.* Which groups of people are you uncomfortable bringing into the church?

5. What would it take for you to trust God that if you bring them in, God can be trusted to "clean them up?"

6. Decide on one loving thing you will do this week for someone you are uncomfortable with. How will you show them God's love and acceptance?

    How will you prepare for this step of faith?

The Power of Peace

To daily and effectively put on the helmet of salvation, the breastplate of righteousness and the shield of faith, to expertly wield the sword, doesn't just happen because once we prayed a prayer to ask Jesus to come into our lives. That was only the beginning point. What do we do after that? Read Philippians 4:4-9. List the ways to grow strong in faith mentioned in this passage.

_____ in the Lord.

_____ with everyone, for the Lord is near.

_____; instead pray with thanksgiving.

Think about _____

_____

Imitate _____.

When we live this way, what is the result? (See verses 7 and 9b.)

_____ will guard your _____;

and the _____ will _____.

These verses show us that _____ is powerful; they also show us how to live it. How will living this way make us more effective for the Kingdom?

Why do you think it is important for *both* our hearts and minds to be protected?

How will filling our minds with God's Word help to fulfill Paul's instruction in verse 8?

How will following Paul's instructions help you to wield the sword?

How will you put on the breastplate of righteousness this week?

The Heart of the Matter

Meditate on the following scriptures:

"And this is my prayer: that your love may abound more and more in knowledge and depth of insight, so that you may be able to discern what is best and may be pure and blameless...filled with the fruit of righteousness that comes through Jesus Christ..."

(Philippians 1:9-11)

"If you have any encouragement from being united with Christ, if any comfort from his love, if any fellowship with the Spirit, if any tenderness and compassion...[be] like-minded..."

(Philippians 2:1-2)

"Christ's love compels us..."

(II Corinthians 5:14)

"Love must be sincere...Be devoted to one another...Bless those who persecute you...Rejoice with those who rejoice; mourn with those who mourn. Live in harmony...If it is possible, as far as it depends on you, live at peace with everyone...Let no debt remain outstanding, except the continuing debt to love one another...Love does no harm [and] is the fulfillment of the law."

(Romans 12:9-18; 13:8, 10)

"A tree is recognized by its fruit...For out of the overflow of the heart the mouth speaks."

(Matthew 12:33b, 34b)

"Jesus replied, 'Love the Lord your God with all your heart and with all your soul and with all your mind... Love your neighbor as yourself.'"

(Matthew 22:37-39)

"Stop judging by mere appearances, and make a right judgment."

(John 7:24)

"Who are you to judge someone else's servant? To his own master he stand or falls. And he will stand, for the Lord is able to make him stand...Make up your mind not to put any stumbling block or obstacle in your brother's way."

(Romans 14:4,13)

How important is the heart?

What is the difference between a mind that is filled with God's Word and a heart and mind filled with God's Word?

How does God's Word become more to us than "the letter that kills?"

Praying in the Spirit

1. We are to pray in the Spirit *all the time*. How do you think this is possible?

2. Who and what are we to pray for?

   Mt. 5:44: _____

   Luke 11:2-4: _____

   Mark 11:24: _____

   Luke 10:2 _____

   Mark 14:38: _____

   II Thessalonians 3:1: _____

   I Timothy 2:1-2: _____

   Hebrews 13:15: _____

   James 5:13-16: _____

3. Spend some time evaluating your own prayer life. How much time do you spend on praise and thanksgiving?

   How much time do you spend praying for others rather than yourself?

   The above list is only a partial list of ways we are to pray. Can you think of others? Write them here.

4. What will you do to move closer to praying in the Spirit at all times?

Letting God Fight Our Battles: Navigating Troubled Relationship Waters

It would be easy for me to live at peace with everyone, feeling peace in my heart, if people would just do things my way! Just get out of my way! Just think about me for a change! Just be reasonable! But life is not like that, is it?

This earth is full of turmoil: wars and rumors of wars; marriages disintegrating, children running away from home; brothers and sisters not speaking to each other; parents disowning their children; lifelong friendships ended by a single thoughtless act; freeway drivers and abruptly-terminated workers shooting out their powerlessness and rage with handguns; bombs intentionally set off in markets and day care centers and weddings to make a political statement. It seems that we humans are much better at causing strife than ending it.

Even when we are doing our best to live a life of love, there will be moments, or perhaps long seasons, in our lives when we are in conflict with someone, and that someone may be a person we love. When personal conflict threatens to overwhelm us with fear, grief and anxiety, how do we make sense of things? How do we persevere in our faith, and stay grounded in God?

When Others Act the Enemy

When others act the enemy, the fear and dread we feel tend to diminish our faith and cloud our vision. We look around and try to bring the terrifying situation under some kind of control. That is what King Jehoshaphat did. That desire to control things can cause additional troubles.

Jehoshaphat starts out well. His heart is "devoted to the ways of the Lord" (II Chronicles 17:6). God has blessed him with wealth and power as king of Judah. But then he looks around and sees that little Judah is surrounded by unfriendly nations. He decides on a commonly-accepted approach: through marriage, he allies himself with the king of Israel, Ahab.

What could be wrong with that? Ahab is king of the nation of Israel, God's chosen people. To our human way of thinking, it seems like the perfect solution. The problem is two-fold: first of all, Ahab does not value God's take on things; second of all, Jehoshaphat (let's just call him "Josh"

121

for short) is so eager to please Ahab, that he ends up giving up his efforts to determine God's will, and follows Ahab's lead. This is how it all goes down:

When Ahab's "prophets," chosen because they tell him what he wants to hear (II Chronicles 18:1-17), encourage Ahab to go to war, "Josh" wants to consult a real prophet, that is, someone who hears from God and has the courage to speak it out. That prophet, Micaiah, is summoned to appear before the kings of Israel and Judah. He could never be accused of beating around the bush or being subtle. There is no doubt about what his message means. He says, "I saw all Israel scattered on the hills like sheep without a shepherd, and the Lord said, 'These people have no master. Let each one go home in peace'" (18:16).

What amazing courage! He is looking into the face of the king and saying, "In the Lord's eyes, you are not the king of Israel." He further states that the course of action should be peace, not war. Ahab whines about the fact that this prophet never prophesies to the king's liking; Micaiah elaborates further: "All your prophets are lying to you; you will choose to believe them. This venture will result in utter disaster." As thanks for his words of truth, he is thrown into prison.

Josh and Ahab go out to battle. Ahab is killed. Josh is told by Jehu the seer, "Should you help the wicked and love those who hate the Lord?" (19:1-3)

Josh appears to accept this correction and learn from it. He goes back to depending on God. When several neighboring kings gather to make war against him, it becomes a test of his resolve to depend on God, even in trying circumstances: Will he now choose to rely on God? He calls all the people to an assembly, and prays an impassioned plea for God to intervene. "We do not know what to do, but our eyes are on you" (20:12). This is the first thing to do when conflict, or the threat of conflict, arises in our lives: **_Pray._**

Then they simply **_wait in His presence, until God speaks_**. This is the second thing. Most often there are principles already laid down in the Word that apply directly to your situation. The important thing is to depend on God by: 1) praying; 2) waiting; 3) listening; and 4) obeying.

Jehoshophat has been corrected and rebuked by God for his independence and self-reliance in the past. _Now, instead of becoming angry, rebellious and bitter, he learns to humbly walk in God's counsel when things are stressful, and to conform himself to God's will._

This love for God has _cost_ him. He has had to give up an earthly show of strength and swift action, qualities that we admire in our leaders. He has given that up for quiet obedience. In a crisis, he shows that his love for God is not only costly, but also _accountable_. He answers to God for his people, and he answers to the people for his choice in how to lead them as their king.

He now knows how to do both the _giving and receiving_ that true relationship requires. He gives up the temptation to act immediately in a show of force as a king who has spent his entire reign keeping a strong and large contingent of fighting men trained and positioned throughout the kingdom. He gives up his right to act on his own authority as king of Judah. He gives all power and authority to God in this emergency; he gives up any claim to wisdom or knowledge, and opens himself up completely to receiving from God everything he needs to combat this threat.

His love for God is more than costly and accountable, and it involves more than giving and receiving: it *speaks the truth*, and it is *humbly grateful*. We know that by his words and actions in a time when he is under extreme stress. He cries out to God, "O Lord, God of our fathers...You rule! Did you not drive out the inhabitants of this land before your people and give it to [them] forever?" (20:5-9) He declares the truth that earthly kings appear powerful, but God himself is the true ruler "over all the kingdoms of the nations." He shows his gratitude by speaking out again what God has already done for his people.

He shows complete humility and dependence on God: "O our God...we have no power to face this vast army that is attacking us. We do not know what to do, but our eyes are on you" (verse 12).

This is another of those prayers worth adopting as our own. When we feel attacked, it is time to cry out, **"O God! You are the King of the Universe, and You are the King of my heart. You have blessed me in the past and now I am in trouble. I have no power to make it go away, and I don't know what to do. But my eyes are on You."**

Then stand before Him and wait. That's what the entire nation of Judah did. They just stood and waited. We don't know how long they waited, just that it was long enough. God spoke through one of the Levites standing in the crowd, and oh, they had to know it was God! It had the sound and feel of the Father's heart:

"This is what the Lord says to you: Do not be afraid or discouraged because of this vast army. For the battle is not yours, but God's...Stand firm and see the deliverance the Lord will give you. Do not be afraid; do not be discouraged. Go out to face them tomorrow, and the Lord will be with you" (verses 15-17).

And all the people fell down, thousands upon tens of thousands, hundreds and hundreds of thousands, fell down in that place and worshiped the Warrior God who protects and defends His people.

After God miraculously defeated Judah's enemies, "The fear of God came upon all the kingdoms of the countries when they heard how the Lord had fought against the enemies of Israel. And the kingdom of Jehoshophat was at peace, for his God had given him rest on every side" (20:29-30).

Are you in a battle? Feeling threatened or attacked? It has been said that "Sorrow looks back; worry looks around; faith looks up." Look up, take a deep breath, and relax into your Father's heart. Hide yourself in Him. Ask Him to be with you in this, to give you wisdom and guidance; acknowledge that you are totally dependent on Him. When God wins the battle, there is rest.

Thank you for being my Warrior God! Come to my rescue! My eyes are on You.

Dealing with Confrontation

Our God came to this earth in the form of a baby, and the angels called out, "Peace to men of good will!" He is the Prince of Peace. His work on earth is to restore peace between God and man, and between men. "There are six things the Lord hates, seven that are detestable to him: haughty eyes, a lying tongue, hands that shed innocent blood, a heart that devises wicked schemes, feet that are quick to rush into evil, a false witness who pours out lies and a man who stirs up dissension among brothers" (Proverbs 6:16-19). All of these things the Lord hates are thought up and acted out out of a heart that does not seek the good of his neighbor, or even his brother.   All of these things create the opposite of the peace that is so dear to God's heart.

"A haughty tongue" results from an attitude of superiority. "Pride only breeds quarrels," we read in Proverbs 13:10, "but *wisdom is found in those who take advice*." When advice is given to us, *we would be wise to be open to it*. It doesn't mean that we have to take all advice without consideration; that would be as foolish as rejecting all advice. When someone confronts us, and does it with an attitude of concern for our well-being, God's Word says repeatedly that we are to **humbly receive advice and correction**. If we are too proud and self-confident to consider the possibility that the advice is from God, we may create quarrels and misunderstandings, and we may create grief for ourselves down the road.

God hates "a lying tongue;" this is one of the most common ways a confrontation or rift begins between us. If you are confronted by someone whom you have lied about, or lied to, you are being confronted by God, and the wise response is repentance. How seldom that happens! The Word is clear: if you want to be in right relationship with God, become a truth-teller. Lies create nothing but trouble. Humble yourself in the presence of God and in the presence of your wronged brother or sister, and admit your fault. Having a "lying tongue" implies that lying has become a pattern, a major coping skill, a habit. It will take determination and prayer, but anyone who belongs to Christ and realizes he has a lying tongue can turn, repent, and **learn to speak the truth.**

"Hands that shed innocent blood" are obviously sinful hands. It's easy to skip right over this, because we think it doesn't apply to us. But God's Word cautions us that "as a man thinks in his heart, so is he." Our thoughts and words have tremendous power to affect us when we dwell on them and rehearse them. I John 3:14, 15 makes God's perspective on this clear: "Anyone who does not love remains in death. Anyone who hates his brother is a murderer, and you know that no murderer has eternal life in him." When we are angry, when we are confronted about some perceived wrong, or when we want to confront someone about their wrongdoing toward us, we need to pay attention to our thoughts.

If we entertain imaginations of vengeance, doing the other person harm, committing sins against them, we are practicing in our minds what we think we would never do: shedding innocent blood. True crime shows are full of examples of previously law-abiding citizens becoming enraged over some affront, plotting a crime against the one they resent, becoming consumed with a destructive course of action and then carrying it out, feeling justified and righteous. "Vengeance is mine," says the Lord. "I will repay." Let God fight this battle. It is not your job. Dwelling on angry, resentful thoughts will damage your relationship with God and with others. Instead, look for the positive, the hopeful, and dwell on these things, as you commit your problems to a God who knows what to do.

"A heart that devises wicked schemes" is a heart that does not concern itself with the best interests of his neighbor. It is a heart in which the emotions and will and intentions are motivated only by self-interest. It is a heart that shuts out God and puts self on the throne. When we find ourselves seriously devising ways to hurt or take advantage of others, God says, "prepare your minds for action; be self-controlled; set your hope fully on the grace to be given you when Jesus Christ is revealed. As obedient children, do not conform to the evil desires you had when you lived in ignorance. But just as he who called you is holy, so be holy in all you do; for it is written: 'Be holy, because I am holy' (I Peter 1:13-16).

"Feet that are quick to rush into evil" are motivated by a heart that has cut itself off from compassion and conscience. When we impulsively act out of anger, selfishness, greed or jealousy, we are in danger of rushing into evil. Again, it is not our job to punish the evil done against us. "For it is God's will that *by doing good* you should silence the ignorant talk of foolish men. Live as free men, but do not use your freedom as a cover-up for evil; live as servants of God. Show proper respect to everyone" (I Peter 2:15-17).

God hates "a false witness who pours out lies." There are many ways to lie, and we are only lying to ourselves if we think a "little white lie," or giving a false impression, is not a lie. Other lies might be, for example, allowing an inaccurate statement, an unfair judgment or bit of gossip to stand unchallenged. We will get good at what we practice. If we practice avoiding confrontation or getting our way by not being completely honest, we are practicing deceit, and we are not pleasing God. "Whoever would love life and see good days must keep his tongue from evil and his lips from deceitful speech. He must turn from evil and do good; he must seek peace and pursue it. For the eyes of the Lord are on the righteous and his ears are attentive to their prayer, but the face of the Lord is against those who do evil" (Psalms 34:12-16). Being a false witness implies that someone else is going to experience judgment and suffer consequences if the witness is believed. It may be in a court of law, or it may be in the court of public opinion. God hates a false witness, someone who leads others to believe a lie about another person. I want to be a truth-teller.

"A man who stirs up dissension among brothers" is not in good standing with God. It's the gentle answer that God commends, not harsh words (Proverbs 15:1). You can be the "hot-tempered man [that] stirs up dissension," or you can **be the "patient [one who] calms a quarrel"** (Proverbs 15:18). "A fool gives full vent to his anger, but a wise man keeps himself under control" (Proverbs 29:11). Sometimes dissension is stirred up without *obvious* anger at its root. It can be very subtle. People may be fooled by manipulations that create dissension and disconnection, but God is not. He hates the unchecked deceitfulness of the human heart, for it inevitably pits us against each other, and destroys our ability to know the truth from a lie. To move from our heart's natural deceitfulness to a place of honor and integrity and godly character, we must continually walk in connection to God and humbly acknowledge that we are dependent on Him for our goodness and our growth.

We don't like confrontation or conflict. We tend to either run from it, shut down and refuse to engage in any way, or we try to be stronger, louder and "right" in order to win. None of these natural reactions is pleasing to God. It's not the conflict that is the problem; it's our reaction to it. What feels like confrontation may actually be wisdom presented to us, a truth we have been blind to. Conflict sometimes brings to light problems that need to be dealt with, misunderstandings that need to be cleared up, or hurts that need to be tended to. **Conflict is an opportunity to ask good questions.** In order to get the information we need to solve a problem, we need to ask the right questions, to have curiosity about the dilemma and the other person involved. While we need to communicate, we should avoid flooding the other person with a torrent of words. "He who holds his tongue is wise" (Proverbs 10:19).

It's an interesting fact that a truly wise person, instead of being proud of his wisdom, is humble. That's because humility *actually comes from* wisdom (James 3:13). James describes wisdom as "pure, peace-loving, considerate, submissive, full of mercy and good fruit, impartial and sincere. Peacemakers who sow in peace raise a harvest of righteousness" (3:17-18). If we **keep in mind that our goal is peace**, we can go into a conflict situation with a sincere desire to restore a good relationship. Our goal is not to be proven right; our goal is not to win; our goal is not to avoid all conflict; our goal is not to exhibit our superior prowess with either the deft use of words or to silence the other with the sheer number of words we can say on a subject. Our goal is, instead, the restoration of peace and healthy relationship.

No matter how wise and humble and sincere any two people are, if they have enough interactions, at some point, there will be a difference of opinion, a misunderstanding, or a perceived offense. "If your brother sins against you, go and show him his fault, just between the two of you. If he listens to you, you have won your brother over. But if he will not listen, take one or two others along, so that every matter may be established by the testimony of two or three witnesses" (Matthew 18:15-16). "And when you stand praying, if you hold anything against anyone, forgive him, so that your Father in heaven may forgive you your sins;" "Judge not, that you be not judged;" "So when you offer your gift to God at the altar, and you remember that your brother or sister has something against you, leave your gift there at the altar. Go and make peace with that person, and then come and offer your gift"(Mark 11:25, Mt 7:1, Mt 5:23). One way or another, as soon as you are aware that there is something wrong in a relationship, you must **do your part to fix the problem**, for "we are all members of one body. Be kind and compassionate to one another" (Ephesians 4:25, 32).

If both parties are willing to discuss the issue, the reason for the misunderstanding will likely be uncovered, and both can understand how it happened. The Word cautions us to take care with the manner in which we share our position. "There is one whose rash words are like sword thrusts, but the tongue of the wise brings healing" (Proverbs 12:18). Our attitude can make all the difference in how we are received. "Pride only leads to arguments, but those who take advice are wise" (Proverbs 13:10).

Lord, teach me ways of responding to confrontation and defusing conflict that honor You, and strengthen the Body. Be my guide and teacher. Amen.

126

When conflict occurs in the Body of Christ, how we deal with it is of major importance. It makes the difference between drawing others to Christ, or repelling them. Jesus made it clear: "By this [love] will all men know you are my disciples." If, instead of love, others see ugly disagreements, "turf" disputes, resentments, power struggles, envy, and gossip, the Body of Christ looks just like the world, and not all that attractive.

We have a serious problem, folks! The Word is very clear about how we are supposed to relate to each other. "Take note of this: Everyone should be quick to listen, slow to speak and slow to become angry, for man's anger does not bring about the righteous life that God desires" (James 1:19-20). "Speak and act as those who are going to be judged by the law that gives freedom, because judgment without mercy will be shown to anyone who has not been merciful. Mercy triumphs over judgment!" (James 2:12-13). Be completely humble and gentle; be patient, bearing with one another in love" (Ephesians 4:2).

We live like this until someone really aggravates us. Then all that Christlikeness tends to go out the window, and we do what we do best: royally mess things up. And that's why we need forgiveness. That's also why we need to forgive.

So what is forgiveness anyway? There are four New Testament types of forgiveness:

1. *aphiemi,* "to send away" (signifies a complete removal of the debt, including the cause of the offense). This is "forgive and forget" forgiveness; but there are conditions.
2. *charizomai,* "to bestow a favor unconditionally;" the idea here is that everything lost is redeemable.
3. *apoluo,* "to dismiss any claim: you don't owe me anything."
4. *paresis,* "overlooking on the basis of ignorance or innocence," and the similar, *anechomai,* "to bear with, endure, forbear, suffer."

New Testament forgiveness is radical: We are to forgive sins, just like God forgives sin. **We are *commanded* to forgive; it is not an optional grace.** In fact, Jesus makes it clear that God's forgiveness of our sins, when we ask, depends on our forgiving the offenses of others against us. This is serious business. And it's not easy. Oswald Chambers comments, "We talk glibly about forgiving when we have never been injured; when we are injured, we know that it is not possible, apart from God's grace, for one human being to forgive another."

The first thing we need to do is to get rid of the notion that this is humanly possible! This is possible only so far as we are connected to Christ, actively choosing to forgive, and depending on the power of the Holy Spirit to make us able: to bear with each other, to erase the offense, to bestow grace upon one another.

When we are able to forgive, it is a miracle to praise God for! It is a miracle we need over and over again; it is a necessary miracle. D. Martyn Lloyd-Jones says, "I say to the glory of God and in utter humility that whenever I see myself before God and realize even something of what my blessed Lord has done for me, I am ready to forgive anybody anything."

This is the key to learning to forgive well: a constant awareness of our indebtedness to Christ, and also of his mercy and grace toward us in the face of our undeservedness. "He who has been forgiven much, loves much." We have *all* been forgiven much; we just need to recognize and remember it.

It is not enough to be associated with Christ, to study forgiveness, to follow the steps, to say the words. We must have His Life flowing through us, and it requires going back for more over and over again.

At a moment of conflict, when one person may feel unworthy, judged or discouraged, and the other may be hurt, angry or anxious for reassurance, we can make things worse so easily! But this is an opportunity to work the works of God.

Do you remember what it felt like the first moment you realized that God had forgiven your sins, and you knew that you were accepted and loved by God? *God has given us a ministry of giving that away to each other: to make it as if the offense had never occurred.* This is a precious gift.

It has been said that all communication is either an SOS or a bouquet of flowers. If we see clearly that this person is both loved by God, and in need of God's love, we can then cooperate with His work in all humility, patience and obedience. We are to focus on our own limits rather than those of others, and take steps toward peacemaking and forgiveness, then leave the results of our efforts to God.

Forgiveness, reconciliation, relationship, redemption: this is the work of God, the very heart of God. When you are yearning for restoration of good relationship, it is God's own hopeful, generous heart you feel. When we come to one another with our hands and hearts wide open, we are walking on holy ground.

When Others Act the Enemy

1. Think of some situations you have faced when it felt as if someone else was your enemy. What emotions did you have?

    How did you try to control these situations?

    Were these conflicts resolved? If so, how?

2. Think of a conflict situation you are facing right now, or one in the past that was never resolved. Describe it here.

3. Read II Chronicles 20:2-12. Ask at least one other person to join you in prayer for your unresolved conflict situation. Thank God for answered prayer in the past, and ask Him to give you wisdom and guidance to know how to repair relationships in a way that honors and pleases Him. Wait in His presence. Write down any ideas or insights here. Check them against the Word.

4. When you have a clear sense of what to do, follow through in obedience, and write down what happened.

Dealing With Confrontation

1. Ask God to show you what you do or don't do that makes conflict more likely. Take some time and wait in His presence. Reflect on past conflicts, and see if you gain any insights. Write down what you realize about yourself.

2. Think about what you say to yourself, about yourself or about others, when a conflict arises. For example, do you think, *This always happens to me. Everyone is against me.* Or perhaps, *Why does this keep happening to me. I just can't do anything right.* What is the fear, anxiety, or judgment that you make, at the moment you realize there is a problem between you and someone else?

3. Decide on a statement to put in its place that is based on God's Word about who you and others are to Him. Write it down here.

4. Imagine a conflict that has happened, or that could happen. Imagine what is said between you and the other person. Now imagine yourself thinking the statement you created above. What effect does it have on you to think that way in this imaginary conflict?

5. *We don't like confrontation or conflict. We tend to either run from it, shut down and refuse to engage in any way, or we try to be stronger, louder and "right" in order to win. None of these natural reactions is pleasing to God. It's not the conflict that is the problem; it's our reaction...*

    What is the way in which you tend to automatically respond to conflict?

    How has that worked for you?

    Are you ready to work with God to help you find a new way that pleases God and has better results?

6. Whatever the reason for conflict, we must do our part to reconcile with the person we are at odds with. What are some specific actions you can see yourself trying in a conflict to resolve it?

The Forgiving Heart

1. Bring to mind a person you have a troubled relationship with. Take a moment to ask God to show you what attitude He wants you to bring to this situation.

2. Picture this person in your mind. What emotional reaction to you have?

3. Imagine you are writing a letter to this person. You are not going to send it, so you don't have to worry about how it will be received, or if you are explaining yourself well. Just write, and pour out your thoughts.

4. What do you notice about what is in your heart?

5. Ask God to speak to you about this person, and about yourself. If God reproves you, it is because you are His child, and He wants you to grow up to be just like Him! Wait in His presence, and write down what comes to you.

6. Read Mark 11:25. When are we to forgive?

7. Which type of forgiveness do you need toward the person above?
    aphiemi: "forgive and forget"   *charizomai*: unconditional grace
    apoluo: removal of debt   *paresis*: overlooking an offense because of ignorance

Ask God to make you able to forgive.

"Anyone who claims to be in the light but hates his brother is still in darkness." (I John 2:9)

131

Radical Forgiveness

New Testament forgiveness is radical. At the time of Christ, it was believed that only God could forgive sins. Christ openly forgiving sins caused quite a stir; they had no idea just how radical it was going to get. What is the most radical part of New Testament forgiveness? We forgive sins just like God.

1. Who are we to forgive? (Ephesians 4:25, 32, Mark 11:25)

2. Why do we need to forgive? (Mark 11:25, II Corinthians 2:10-11, Ephesians 4:2-3, James 2:1-13)

3. What should we forgive? (Colossians 3:13-15, Luke 17:3-4)

4. How are we to forgive? (James, 2:12-13, James 3:13-18, I Timothy 1:5-11, Ephesians 4:15, Ephesians 4:29, II Corinthians 10:5)

5. How do you think self-reliance, perfectionism, self-loathing, victimhood, fear of getting hurt and long-lasting guilt interfere with forgiveness?

6. How do justifications (I'm only human; Nobody's perfect; I'm not as bad as _____) interfere with forgiveness?

Forgiveness for Dummies: The "How To" Manual

List these *How To Handle Conflict* instructions for the One Offended:

1. Leviticus 19:17-18 _____

2. Luke 17:3-4 _____

3. Matthew 18:15-17 _____

How to Handle Conflict instructions for the Offender:

1. James 1:19-20 _____

2. Matthew 7:1-5 _____

3. Matthew 5:23-24 _____

4. James 5:16 _____

Which of the above aspects of resolving conflict have you demonstrated in the past?

Which ones are hardest for you?

Is forgiveness optional? Explain.

**What do we do when we think we have forgiven someone, but the hurt and resentment keep coming back?

**Is forgiveness instantaneous (a decision) or is it ongoing (a process)?

The Limits of Forgiveness

1. Jesus instructs us to "Love your neighbor as yourself." How does this relate to forgiveness?

2. Is forgiveness a "free pass" to continue on the same path? Explain your thinking.

3. Does forgiving mean we always stay in a relationship and forgive, no matter what?

4. Does God's forgiveness have limits? Explain.

5. Explain how the scriptural principles in the following passages relate to forgiveness:

    John 2:24-25 _____

    Matthew 10:16 _____

    Matthew 18:15-17 _____

    Luke 7:44-49 _____

    Matthew 7:1-5 _____

**Where does the power to forgive come from?

**How do you think a person gets good at forgiveness?

**Who benefits from forgiveness?

**How does the following quote relate to conflict and forgiveness?

"Whatever men expect, they soon come to think they have a right to; the sense of disappointment can, with very little skill on our part, be turned into a sense of injury."
(C.S. Lewis, <u>Screwtape Letters</u>)

The Holy City: When the Walls are Broken Down

Nehemiah's mission to rebuild the broken down walls of Jerusalem began because he wanted to know the truth about the state of the abandoned city. He was willing to face reality, even if it was uncomfortable and distressing, even if it meant that there was work to be done. He asked good questions, questions that had grim answers. He wanted to know the condition of the Jews in exile, and he wanted to know about the holy city, Jerusalem. The answers were not pretty. He had to sit down at the news. He wept. For days he prayed and fasted, and mourned before his God. What a man of faith and character. What a heart.

When he received bad news, he ran straight to the One who has the power and authority, the will and the love, to do more than we could ever ask or think. Nehemiah's powerful, passionate prayer is recorded in Nehemiah 1:5-11.

Oh, understand this: You are God's holy city. The walls, your boundaries, provide you with security, safety, and clear limits. They also provide protection for you, and clear lines for others to observe about what is theirs and what is yours. The walls keep the inside of the city different and set apart from what lies outside the walls.

When disaster has invaded our walls, and we realize the damage, we, too, must run to the One who knows how to put us back together again. If you have experienced abandonment or neglect, physical, verbal, sexual or emotional abuse, if you have experienced rape, abortion, betrayal, breast cancer, infidelity or divorce, the death of a parent, child or spouse, or any other trauma that has gone down deep to the core of you, and changed your idea of who you are, the strength of your walls has been compromised. When the walls of the city have been damaged or destroyed, anyone can see into the city, identify its vulnerabilities, and even come in and out at will.

Nehemiah saw that the gates of Jerusalem had been destroyed by fire; this is a picture for us of some out-of-control power, passion or pretense that starts out looking beautiful and even providing warmth, but ends up creating disaster and dysfunction and destruction.

Look at your city. Has there been an attack, or a natural disaster? Then **you must inspect the walls, and be honest about the damage.** Be courageous like Nehemiah. Face the truth. Nehemiah personally took a good look at every inch of wall, and he went into the darkness to do it. If you refuse to see the damage, you will never set about repairing it.

At first, Nehemiah's work is solitary, but once he realizes that something is wrong and he can't fix it by himself, he collaborates with others, lets them in on what he knows, and gives them the power and opportunity to help him rebuild the walls. He says to the builders, "We will no longer be in disgrace." Broken-down walls result in shame. To banish shame, we must rebuild.

Immediately there is opposition. There always will be. When we begin to rebuild and become strong and protected again, it is a threat to the enemy; when God's people get rid of their shame, get healthy, get busy, Satan doesn't like it. Sometimes there are people that don't like it, either. Nehemiah faced opposition, and so will we, whenever we are doing a work approved by the King. Nehemiah faced anger, ridicule, insults, threats, plotting, and the fear that all of this predictably caused in the workers.

Nehemiah did what was necessary to ensure that the work proceeded:

- He listened, and took the threats seriously.
- He prayed, and posted guards.
- He instructed the builders to build with one hand and have a weapon in the other, so the work could proceed.
- He made it clear that, even though they were armed, their trust was in God.
- Instead of spending his time and strength answering each threat and accusation, he spent his time praying for strength, and stayed focused on the work.

Nehemiah and his dedicated work crew experienced crazy success! The wall was completed against all odds in only 52 days. It was such a miraculous event that even unbelievers gave God the glory. God can do an amazing healing work in you, too. With the walls strong and impenetrable, the gates in place, the storerooms restored at the gates, purification and celebration began in earnest, and in charge of the whole city: a leader chosen for two qualities, integrity and fear of God.

You **have been set in charge of your holy city.** You will keep your city safe, your walls strong, your storehouses full, and your gates functioning to open and close appropriately, only by maintaining your integrity and your reverence for God. Unlawful intrusions, in the form of unhealthy relationships, will deplete your storehouses of blessing: your health, integrity, security, strength, joy, intuition, discretion, self-control. Should your own will or wisdom fail you, your fear of God and knowledge of His Word will serve as a back-up gatekeeper. That's why **the work can only proceed with dependence on God and immersion in His Word:**

- Take every chance to hear the Word, read it, pray it, and live it out (Nehemiah 8).
- Celebrate the sacred (Nehemiah 8:9).
- Appreciate the simple, good things God has given us richly to enjoy (verse 12).
- Let there be a time to end the grieving over what has been lost, to move into joy, for the joy of the Lord truly is our strength.
- Bless others, and share out of a grateful, generous heart (v. 12).
- Gather together with other believers, for celebration, consecration, confession of sin, worship and remembrance of the goodness of God (chapter 9).
- Ask God for blessing, in spite of all your sad history and all your failings. None of that changes God's love for you. He sees you beautiful.

If your walls and gates have been damaged, if your storerooms have been depleted and robbed, there are many ways it could show in your personality. You might be overly quick to react or overreact to even the possibility of a problem, with anger, a torrent of tears, bolting immediately, refusing to speak, or accusing and attacking. You might be too trusting and connect too quickly with others, or you might have put up such strong walls of protection that you cannot fully connect with others. You might forgive and forget too quickly, and therefore allow one person to raid your city of its strength and power and beauty over and over again; or you might hold such grudges that at the merest infraction, you cut off good, important relationships.

Sometimes we ourselves cannot figure out what the problem is; all we know is that the same bad thing keeps happening to us. We may be over-responsible or overly passive or controlling; we may be overly intense or seem detached and snobbish; we just can't see it. If someone else makes a judgment about who we are that we know is inaccurate, it can be helpful to ask questions instead of becoming defensive. The interpretation of your behavior or manner may be incorrect, but finding out how you come across can help you figure out what you are doing that keeps the negative pattern going in your life.

It is generally in conflict that our ability to cope breaks down, and the damage to our city is more obvious. Admit what is there, and, finding wisdom in His Word, seek God for guidance in becoming the person God created you to be. Many times godly counsel can set your course when you yourself don't know how to begin.

One night, lying in the dark, saying goodnight to the Lord, I was troubled about a rift in a relationship. I murmured aloud, "Really there is very little under my control." Immediately I felt in my spirit God say, *Just put one foot in front of the other, and trust Me.* I began to meditate on this deceptively simple instruction.

All I am responsible for is this one step in this one moment. How am I taking this step? With what intention? In what direction? Does it take me closer to God? Closer to others? Does it reflect to others that God is good? Does it reveal His character? Am I taking it in complete dependence on God instead of depending on doing it right or excelling at it? Am I trusting Him in taking the step, and also for the results?

This is really enough to be responsible for! I don't need to take on any more. This is good for us all. "Everyone should carry his own burden" (Galatians 6:5). We don't get there by church-y piety or the appearance of a perfectly positive attitude every moment. No, God wants us to be real, authentic, honest, transparent. A genuine human is a messy one.

Look at David. He is called a man after God's own heart, but at one point he cries out to God in fury about his enemies, "Let their little ones be dashed against the rocks." Now hopefully I will never be squeezed in life's press hard enough to feel that way, but David was, and he didn't pretend otherwise. In that moment that's who he was, and he was so transparent that he actually said it to God, and it was written down, and forever God, and everybody else, knows it.

But here's the thing: In that moment of raw, real emotion, David had this homing pigeon in his heart that, even while he screamed out his hurt and rage, was circling back home, to God. That's what God sees and loves: a heart that finds it place of hope and rest, comfort and provision in Him.

Learning appropriate boundaries (what is my job; what is your job; what is God's job) is at the core of being a force for good in the world. We are not responsible for other people's choices, what they do with what we give them. That is their choice. We are not responsible for the results; that's up to God. We may not like it, but He allows everyone, by virtue of free will, to reject, not appreciate, not believe, not receive, to miss out.

We are responsible only for what we give out, and the intention of our hearts in the giving. If we are breathing out to others love, wisdom, hope, power, joy, peace, we are allowing the free flow of that river, the character, the very nature, of God, through us to others.

Satan does not accept God's sovereignty and he does not accept and respect the boundaries of anyone, yours, mine or God's. That is why we have a war to fight, against "principalities and powers." The skirmishes in the fields do not determine the final outcome, but in the name of the legitimate King, we claim this territory as already His.

Will we sometimes have to firmly set boundaries with people? Absolutely. Even Christ did that, in one instance by turning the money changers tables over. Was he angry? Yes, He was, and legitimately so. There are times when others are behaving so badly toward us, we will be angry, and we will need to take action. To do this in a God-honoring way, we need wisdom, humility, self-control, and a clear understanding of who our enemy really is.

Becoming angry can be a pivotal moment in our lives. Anger is a signal that we feel our boundaries are not being respected. We have an opportunity to notice what is flowing out in life's squeezing moments. We can acknowledge to God any stubbornness and rebellion, independence, self-reliance, selfishness, fear, anxiety. We can realize if we have some hardness of heart, then let ourselves be broken open before God, allowing the ugliness be washed out by the Word and the Spirit. There is healing and restoration available to us in those moments. We can notice the walls have been breached.

I remember taking my seven-year-old son to the doctor for a wound, a deep puncture wound in one knee. He had hit the ground hard and slid down a rocky slope on bare knees. Little pebbles were embedded deep in the flesh and touching them produced exquisite pain. He needed the doctor.

The wound had to be flushed with a strong stream of disinfectant until the pebbles and dirt were dislodged. He screamed and writhed in pain as the tears rolled down my cheeks and I held him down. His wound required cleansing, and the touch of the physician. Then and only then could healing begin.

Deep wounds require deep cleansing work, not Band-Aids. Let the Great Physician come close. There is pain in healing, but after that comes the growth of new baby-soft skin that is actually tougher than what was there before: a scar. **Pain, cleansing, time, instruction in wisdom, protection and the Master's touch bring restoration and transformation.**

The scar forever shows that there has been an injury here. You are never the same. But the wound has healed. You are wiser now. You see someone else's wound, someone else's pain, and you can now cry for them, not just for yourself.

And **most of all, you know the way to the Master Physician's house.** You know the trip is necessary, and the process will at times be painful. But you know, too, that a wounded heart must be made whole again by its Maker. You can say, "Let's go there together, for Christ came to heal the broken hearted."

God speaks to you today, just as surely as He spoke to Israel about Jerusalem: "O afflicted city, lashed by storms and not comforted, I will build you with stones of turquoise, your foundations with sapphires. I will make your battlements of rubies, your gates of sparkling jewels, and all your walls of precious stones" (Isaiah 54:11-12). "'Though the mountains be shaken and the hills be removed, yet my unfailing love for you will not be shaken, nor my covenant of peace be removed,' says the Lord, who has [soothing, tender] compassion on you [as a mother has with her infant]" (verse 10).

So put one foot in front of the other, and trust Him. He is bringing you into a wide and spacious land, a place of rest and peace and joy and strength. When the necessary walls have been rebuilt, when the beautiful city gates are set in place, when the storerooms are full to overflowing with blessing, then joy and peace will settle over your city to rule there, and you can say with assurance, "Lord, You have assigned me my portion and my cup: You have made my lot secure. The boundary lines have fallen for me in pleasant places; surely I have a delightful inheritance" (Psalms 16:5-6).

O Lord, direct the work of rebuilding my heart and life, in spite of past disaster and trauma. Strengthen my heart and mind and will to complete the work to your glory. I want to be a dazzling, holy city set on a hill that brings glory to You, a city with walls, gates, and storerooms of blessing to pour out to others. You have given me a delightful inheritance. Amen.

The Walls

1. What traumas have you experienced in your life that changed who you are, or changed how you see yourself, or changed how you look at life?

2. What effects did these have on you?

3. Who else can you collaborate with to fix the walls?

4. What role has shame played in damaging the walls?

5. Is there any damage from "fire," that is, something that started out seeming good, but ended up as disaster?

Ask God to give you wisdom and resources to rebuild the walls.

"The Lord...looks with compassion on all [your] ruins; he will make deserts like Eden, wastelands like the garden of the Lord...Awake, awake...clothe yourself with strength"(Isaiah 51:3; 52:1).

Planning the Rebuilding

1. Think for a moment about any opposition you have encountered as you have attempted to move forward, rebuild, change and grow. Present this to God, and follow Nehemiah's lead as you deal with obstacles in your way. How can you in your situation:

   Take the threats seriously?

   Post guards?

   Build and stand watch?

   Trust in God?

   Focus on the work and pray for strength, instead of focusing on the threats and answering each accusation.

2. What has God done for you so far that others have noticed?

3. What have your storerooms been depleted of?

4. How will you partner with God to restore the blessings?

5. Explain exactly what it is you will do to depend on God in each of the following ways:

   Immerse yourself in the Word?

   Celebrate the sacred?

   Appreciate the simple things?

   End the grieving and move into joy?

   Bless others out of a generous heart?

   Assemble together with other believers?

"I am the Lord your God...I have put my words in your mouth and covered you with the shadow of my hand..." (Isaiah 51:15-16)

Inspecting the Damage

1. How have unhealthy relationships damaged you?

2. What negative changes to your personality have developed as a result?

   Have you asked for help with any of this?

3. What feedback have you gotten from others about how you come across?

4. How will you "put one foot in front of the other, and trust Him?"

5. What boundary problems have you struggled with?

6. How comfortable are you with setting boundaries for others?

   Explain how you do this.

7. How comfortable are you with respecting the boundaries set by others?

8. What do you think your anger is a signal of? What will you do about it?

"Burst into songs of joy together, you ruins of Jerusalem, for the Lord has comforted his people, he has redeemed Jerusalem." (Isaiah 52:9)

Collaborating with the City Planner

Present your rebuilding project to the City Planner. Ask Him to help you see what you may have missed. Ask Him for wisdom. Write down your prayer here.

"I the Lord have rebuilt what was destroyed and have replanted what was desolate. I the Lord have spoken, and I will do it"(Ezekiel 36:36).

The Building Contract

Spend some time in God's presence, covenanting with Him to do your part to keep your city pure and strong and ready to bless, as well as to stand against opposition. This requires that you agree to obey God, and that you are clear that His direction is more important than anything else: what you want, someone else's feelings, your fears and anxieties, pressure someone else puts on you. Are you ready to obey Him wholeheartedly, and cooperate with His plan?

Below, write what you will do to allow God to make you ready for further service for Him:

"But now, for a brief moment, the Lord our God has been gracious in leaving us a remnant and giving us a firm place in his sanctuary, and so our God gives light to our eyes and a little relief in our bondage. He has granted us new life to rebuild the house of our God and repair its ruins, and he has given us a wall of protection." (from Ezra 9:8-9)

City Heritage

Spend some time thinking about what heritage of faith you come from or what God has brought you out of, what He has blessed you with so far, how He has seen you through difficulties, what He has taught you, what He is doing in you now, and where you feel He is leading you. Just what is your inheritance in the Lord, this "delightful inheritance?" Meditate on this as you worship and thank God. Write down the elements of this inheritance he promises to His children, and also your specific inheritance as you continue to walk with Him, growing into all that He intends for you to be and do.

"I pray also that eyes of your heart may be enlightened in order that you may know the hope to which he has called you, the riches of his glorious inheritance in the saints, and his incomparably great power for us who believe"(Ephesians 1:18-19).

Winepress to Wellspring: Blessed to Be a Blessing

II Chronicles 21: 4-20 tells the bleak story of Jehoram's reign over Judah. As soon as he succeeded his father to the throne, he put all his own brothers to the sword. His reign was so evil, that one rebellion after another flared up. The king instituted idol worship, and required God's people to participate. Jehoram's ungodliness was destroying his kingdom from within. He was warned by God's Word, but nothing affected him. The weakened nation was attacked next from outside. Finally, the king's health was taken from him; it took two years for him to die what must have been a slow, agonizingly painful death.

"He passed away, to no one's regret, and was buried" (II Chronicles 21:20). Sadder, lonelier words have never been written than these. Can you imagine, after your death, *no one* being sorry you were gone, no one missing you? This is the end of Jehoram, King of Judah. This short, candid sentence tells us a lot about him.

He was incapable of connection, compassion, and conscience. He was not a victim. He became this kind of a person because of many choices, large and small, over time, and because of a refusal to reflect and repent.

The ability to connect **and** ***the willingness to repent*** **are the two characteristics that make us capable of authentic, healthy, intimate relationship, and they are the two characteristics that make it possible for us to leave a legacy, advance the Kingdom, please and obey God, and grow in grace over a lifetime.** It is what makes people cry when we are gone, and rejoice because we are in a far better place after death. These two characteristics, completely lacking in Jehoram, are the two qualities that show us to be made in the very image of God.

The first characteristic, **the ability to connect, comes out of *conscience***, that is, having a clear, heartfelt sense of right and wrong that guides our attitudes and actions, **and *compassion***, that is, being able to put ourselves in another's place and truly care deeply about what they are going through.

If our understanding of right and wrong is primarily intellectual, we will have all the right answers, and we may know how to act and what to say to make others feel cared about, but we will easily ignore their feelings, if paying attention gets in the way of what we want to do. True compassion is unselfish. Counterfeit compassion remains selfish, even while it appears to care, or speaks caring words.

Having a sensitive conscience is costly. We put the old self to death daily and refuse to give in to selfishness. We hold ourselves to a higher standard; we compare ourselves to the Word of God rather than to other human beings.

Being compassionate is also costly. We slow down, take time to listen, when someone is suffering and needs to talk. Instead of interrupting or offering advice, instead of dismissing or minimizing, instead of slapping a Scripture Band-Aid on the problem and walking away, instead of assuming we can identify for the person what it is they are doing wrong that got them into this mess, we simply listen. We pay attention. We ask good questions. We pray with them. We weep with those who weep. We figure out, or find out, what we can do to help. In most cases, just being there is the best gift. You know and keep your separateness, while at the same time caring deeply that hardship has come to another, and it hurts.

Often when people are overwhelmed by their pain, they need support so badly, that simply asking them, "How are you?" in a crowded room is enough for all the pain to start spilling out. I have been there; have you? If you have, you know what typically happens next. You get interrupted or walked away from, and you realize, *Oh, I was just supposed to say "fine," even though I've fallen through thin ice and I'm dying.*

I do not mean to suggest that anyone has the right to hold you hostage while you are deluged with their pain. We all have the right to set our own boundaries, and we do not want to encourage anyone to stay stuck in their pain, dragging us down with them. But, oh, let us set those boundaries with compassion!

God, give us eyes to see the brokenhearted with your heart of compassion. God, grant us the wisdom to know how to handle these delicate moments, offered up to us by a God who cares passionately about each one of us, and longs to see us care deeply about each other.

The second characteristic, **the willingness to reflect and repent, is a requirement for meaningful relationship with both God and each other**. To reflect basically means to intentionally hold up the mirror and admit what it is that we see. This mirror, instead of reflecting back to us the outer appearance, shows us what is on the inside. What's on the inside will leak out, and it will hurt or advance the Kingdom's work. We will only be willing to reflect if we are also willing to repent, because seeing ourselves honestly sometimes means we will see something that does not line up with God's Word and character. When we see a sin, an error, a weakness, a failing, we confess it to the One who always hears, always forgives, always heals.

This ability to reflect on ourselves and repent when necessary requires both honesty and accountability. **Honesty and accountability require us to constantly be in the Word, because**

any other standard we might use to judge ourselves is inadequate and inaccurate. This is our plumb line.

True reflection and repentance based on God's Word will always result in humility and gratitude. We become slow to judge, swift to love. A humble, grateful heart is one that is ready for deep, life-giving relationship; it is a heart that can reflect Christ powerfully to the world.

Keep our hearts sweet, Lord! Keep us yearning deeply for You to be formed in us, for Your Word to be reflected more and more in us. Teach us what it means to be humbly grateful in all our relationships.

The river of His fresh-squeezed Life, the power of His Holy Spirit, is meant to flow abundantly right through us and on out to others. It was never meant to be a meager seasonal trickle that we continually beg for; it was never meant to be dammed up so that we hoard it for ourselves. It's a river of living water! His purpose is to demonstrate Christ through us, to transform us, and to empower us to reflect Christ continually, drawing all to Him.

In order for Christ to be seen, we must give way to the King. We were never meant to be in control of anyone or anything but our own character and choices, and that only by the power of the Holy Spirit. We must allow God to conform us to His image, and enable us to do the works of God, then humbly leave the results to Him.

As we worship Him, read His Word, submit to Him in obedience, our desire for His companionship increases. We spend more time with Him, praying our way through our days. We begin to see His heart, then to feel His heart, then to have His heart. This is the only way to reflect Christ in a healing, restorative, transformational way to others.

His Word in our hands can be the "sword that thrusts," the "letter that kills," unless we are flowing in the stream of that grace-filled Love that is the heart of God. There is no one who is immune to lapses; we will all sometimes fail at this. Throughout scripture, God tells us what we are to do at those times: confess, repent, make things right with our brother or sister, and **keep pressing forward to learn how to work the works of God.**

What are those works of God? They are the opposite of self-satisfied religious observance, and pompous public piety. They have nothing to do with the mere "appearance" of godliness. "They ask me for just decisions and *seem* eager for God to come near them," God says of his people in Isaiah 58:2. Everything looks good on the outside. But God knows their hearts: "On the day of your fasting, you do as you please and exploit all your workers. Your fasting ends in quarreling and strife...You cannot fast as you do today and expect your voice to be heard on high" (from verses 3-4).

"Is not this the kind of fasting I have chosen:

"to **loose the chains of injustice** and untie the cords of the yoke, to set the oppressed free and break every yoke?

"Is it not to **share your food** with the hungry and to provide the poor wanderer with shelter; **when you see the naked, to clothe him**, and **not to turn away** from your own flesh and blood?

"Then your light will break forth like the dawn, and your healing will quickly appear; then your righteousness will go before you and the glory of the Lord will be your rear guard. Then you will call, and the Lord will answer; you will cry for help, and he will say: Here am I.

"If you **do away with** the yoke of **oppression**,

"**with the pointing finger and malicious talk**,

"and **if you spend yourselves** in behalf of the hungry and satisfy the needs of the oppressed,

"then your light will rise in the darkness, and your night will become like the noonday. The Lord will guide you always;

"he will satisfy your needs in a sun-scorched land and will strengthen your frame. You will be like a well-watered garden, like a spring whose waters never fail.

"Your people will rebuild the ancient ruins and will raise up the age-old foundations; you will be called Repairer of Broken Walls, Restorer of Streets with Dwellings.

"If you keep your feet from breaking the Sabbath and from doing as you please on my holy day, **if you call the Sabbath a delight and the Lord's holy day honorable**, and if you honor it by not going your own way and not doing as you please or speaking idle words,

"then you will find your joy in the Lord, and I will cause you to ride on the heights of the land and to feast on the inheritance" (Isaiah 58:6-14).

"When the Son of Man comes in his glory, and all the angels with him, he will sit on his throne in heavenly glory. All the nations will be gathered before him, and he will separate the people one from another as a shepherd separates the sheep from the goats. He will put the sheep on his right and the goats on his left.

"Then the King will say to those on his right, 'Come, you who are blessed by my Father; take your inheritance, the kingdom prepared for you since the creation of the world. For I was hungry and you gave me something to eat. I was thirsty and you gave me something to drink. I was a stranger and you invited me in. I needed clothes and you clothed me. I was sick and you looked after me. I was in prison and you came to visit me.'

"Then the righteous will answer him, 'Lord, when did we see you hungry and feed you, or thirsty and give you something to drink? When did we see you a stranger and invite you in, or needing clothes and clothe you? When did we see you sick or in prison and go to visit you?'

"The King will reply, '**I tell you the truth, whatever you did for one of the least of these brothers of mine, you did for me**'" (Matthew 25:31-40).

This is our "delightful inheritance" in the Lord: to serve Him in obedience, holiness, love, humility, gratitude and joy; to serve Him by serving others. If we live this out, no one will say or think of us after we're gone, "S/he passed away to no one's regret."

Here, Lord, are my hands, my feet, my mind, my heart, soul, strength and time. Here are my tears and the dust of my past. Here is the beauty of what you are building in me. Here am I. Use me. Amen.

"God is love. Whoever lives in love lives in God, and God in him...And he has given us this command: Whoever loves God must also love his brother...Let us not love with words or tongue but with actions and in truth. This then is how we know that we belong to the truth, and how we set our hearts at rest in his presence" (I John 4:16, 21; 3:18-19).

Writing My Mission Statement Part 1

I hope you have grown throughout this study. This is a chance to reflect on who you are and where you want to go from here.

Before we talk about what a mission statement is, first answer these questions; they will be useful later.

Who are you? Who has God created you to be? Who have you become through what you have learned and experienced?

What would you like to accomplish? (What problems or conditions do you have compassion for? What problems or conditions do you want to affect or change? Who do you want to provide opportunities for?)

How do you see yourself doing this? (What gifts, talents, abilities do you believe you have been given?)

What are your values, your guiding principles and beliefs about all of this? (What is most important to you?)

Writing My Mission Statement Part II

The Cheshire Cat, in Lewis Carroll's <u>Alice in Wonderland</u>, wisely commented, "If you don't know where you're going, it doesn't matter which way you go." The opposite is also true: the path you choose determines your destination.

Where do you want to end up? How do you want to be remembered? One way to get in touch with that is to write your own obituary as you would like it to read. What do you want to be true of you? What do you want your "end of the road" to look like here on Planet Earth? Write your own obituary below.

(If you prefer, write instead a speech given at your retirement dinner, telling what you have been appreciated for in the lives of those around you.)

My Mission Statement Part III

The exercise of putting in writing what you are all about can help bring your purpose, vision, goals and life work into greater focus for you.

Refer to the previous pages for help in filling in the blanks.

My Mission Statement

I, _____, as a _____,
         (name)   (who are you?)

purpose to _____, _____,
              (change or accomplish what?)

and _____, through _____,
                                  (actions)

_____, and _____,

because I believe that _____
                              (state your values and guiding principles)

This is your mission statement; continue to refine it as your understanding of your purpose and vision and gifts becomes more clear. May this mission statement help you to navigate your continuing adventure of the "Fresh-Squeezed Life."

Thank you!

for joining me at the Fresh-Squeezed Life Cafe. I hope it has been both refreshing and challenging for you. The good news is that God will always meet you here, whenever you set apart some time to "come away" with Him, have intimate conversation with Him, drink of His Spirit and eat of His Word.

The invitation to fully nourish yourself with this Fresh-Squeezed Life is always open:

"Come with me by yourselves to a quiet place and get some rest" (Mark 6:21). "See! The winter is past; the rains are over and gone. Flowers appear on the earth; the season of singing has come...Arise...come with me" (Song of Songs 2:11, 13).

There is nothing more important. "I count everything as loss compared to the possession of the priceless privilege--the overwhelming preciousness, the surpassing worth and supreme advantage--of knowing Christ Jesus my Lord, and of progressively becoming more deeply and intimately acquainted with Him, of perceiving and recognizing and understanding Him more fully and clearly." (Philippians 3:8, Amplified)

He loves you so much! He has, *"Place[d] [you] like a seal over [His] heart" (Song of Songs 8:6).* He has *"engraved you on the palms of his hands" (Isaiah 49:16).*

"How great is the love the Father has lavished on us that we should be called children of God! " (I John 3:1)

So *"Strengthen the feeble hands, steady the knees that give way; say to those with fearful hearts, 'Be strong, do not fear; your God will come...a highway will be there; it will be called the Way of Holiness...It will be for those who walk in that Way...Only the redeemed will walk there, and the ransomed of the Lord will return...Gladness and joy will overtake them, and sorrow and sighing will flee away" (from Isaiah 35:3-10).*

"Are there those who respect the Lord? He will point them to the best way. They will enjoy a good life, and their children will inherit the land. The Lord tells his secrets to those who respect him." (Psalms 25:12-14, New Century Version)

"The Lord is exalted, for he dwells on high; he will fill Zion with justice and righteousness. He will be the sure foundation for your times, a rich store of salvation and wisdom and knowledge; the fear of the Lord is the key to this treasure." (Isaiah 33:5-6)

Christ has "made us to be a kingdom and priests to serve his God and Father--to him be glory and power for ever and ever! Amen." (Revelation 1:6)

Now "MAY THE GOD OF PEACE, WHO THROUGH THE BLOOD OF THE ETERNAL COVENANT BROUGHT BACK FROM THE DEAD OUR LORD JESUS, THAT GREAT SHEPHERD OF THE SHEEP, EQUIP YOU WITH EVERYTHING GOOD FOR DOING HIS WILL, AND MAY HE WORK IN US WHAT IS PLEASING TO HIM, THROUGH JESUS CHRIST, TO WHOM BE GLORY FOR EVER AND EVER. AMEN." (HEBREWS 13:20-21)

and Amen.